Also by Ruby Gwin

A Day That Would End Tearing at Your Heart

The 250th Field Artillery Men Remember World War II

World War II

In memory

In memory of Walter Irvin and those who made
the supreme sacrifice for the triumph victory
for right over might for their country.

Acknowledgment

Special thanks to Dr. Gilbert and Mary Jo "McKinney" Gutwein and Barbara "McKinney" Kerkhoff and Rolland McKinney for their supply of diary, pictures, and helpful information for their grandfather's Walter "Walt" Irvin's story.

To my publishing team at Trafford Publishing that has been there with me throughout this book's journey—many many thanks.

Nika Corales, Check-in Coordinator

Marvin Edwards, Publishing Consultant

Ryan Gavini, Marketing Consultant

Nick Arden, Publishing Services Associate

Contents

Preface

B Y THE END OF the war, the map of Central Europe during World War I was redrawn into several smaller states. German, Russian, Ottoman, and Austro-Hungarian empires had been military and politically defeated with the Allies victorious. The assassination of Archduke Franz Ferdinand of Austria, the heir to the throne of Austria-Hungary, by a Yugoslav nationalist was the proximate trigger of the war in June 1914. The consequence led Habsburg to an ultimate against the Kingdom of Serbia and spread around to other parts of the world. When the war erupted, the United States attempted to remain neutral as an advocate for the rights of neutral states.

On 28 July 1914, conflicts had opened with the invasion of Serbia by Austro-Hungarian forces, followed by the German invasion of Belgium, Luxembourg, and France. Russia attacked against Germany. On the western front, the German Army carried out a version of the Schlieffen Plan, designed to quickly attack France through neutral Belgium and then encircle the French

Army on the German Border. On 4 August 1914, the execution of the Schieffen Plan led Britain to declare war on Germany.

General Count Alfred von Schlieffen, creator of the Schlieffen Plan, believed that any future war in Europe would be in the western sector. In 1905, Europe had effectively divided into two parts: Germany, Austria, and Italy (Triple Alliance) and Britain, France, and Russia (Triple Entente). Schlieffen, Chief of the German General Staff, regarded France as their most dangerous opponent. With Russia not as advanced in areas such as France, Schlieffen believed it would take at least six weeks for Russia to mobilize their forces and that any possible fighting on the Russian-German border could be coped with for a few weeks while the bulk of German forces could concentrate on France. He orchestrated a massive and surprise attack against France that would be enough to put off the British becoming involved in a continental war. He allowed six weeks into building his plan of a surprise attack against a France campaign to Russia and take on the Russians. His plan assumed that Germany would defeat France in less than six weeks. The plan for attack was to go through Belgium and Luxemburg. Belgium, in 1839, had her neutrality guaranteed by Britain, so his strategy for success depended greatly on Britain not supporting Belgium. There were theaters of conflict among the Central Powers and in the end suffered from miscommunication. The first conflicts of the war in 1914 involved British, French, and German colonial forces in Africa. French and British troops invaded the German protectorate of Togoland. German forces in Southwest Africa attacked South Africa in which irregular intervals of fierce fighting continued for the rest of the war. The German colonial forces in East Africa led by Colonel Paul Emil von Lettow-Vorbeck fought a guerrilla warfare campaign, and not until two weeks after the armistice took effect in Europe that he surrendered. At the outbreak of the war, the Germans were successful, particularly during the *Battle of the Frontiers*. From 5 September through 12 September, the French, with assistance from the British forces, halted the German forces in advance on the eastern side of Paris at the *Battle of the Maine* to end mobile warfare in the west.

After a 1918 offensive attack along the western front, the US forces entered the trenches, and the Allies drove back the German Armies in a series of successful offensives and with Germany revolutionaries' trouble agreed to a ceasefire on 11 November 1918 known as Armistice Day.

On 22 April 1915, during the on-land fighting at Ypres, the Germans used chlorine gas for the first time on the Western Front and forced the Algerian troops to retreat, leaving a four-mile gap opening in the allied lines and this gave the Germans, Kitchener Woods. Canadian soldiers closed the breach during the *Second Battle of Ypres*. At the *Third Battle of Ypres*, Canadian and ANZAC troops took the village of Passchendaele. The first and second battles at Flanders and Verdun were costly and imposed a heavy strain on the Western troops but managed to adapt themselves to the German method of employing counterattacks and imposed a strain for the Germans that prevented Ludendorff from executing the Schlieffen Plan elsewhere.

In the *First Battle of Marne*, both Entente and German forces began a series of outflanking maneuvers in so-called Race to the Seas in order to gain tactical advantages. The Germans had cruisers scattered across the seas that were used to attack allied merchants' shipping. German U-boats attempted to cut off the supply lines between North America and Britain. Attacks came without warning. The United States launched a protest after the sinking of the passenger ship *RMS Lusitania* in 1915. President Wilson called for war on Germany after the sinking of seven US merchant ships by submarines and the publication of the Zimmerman telegram. The US Congress declared war against Germany on April 6, 1917. Germany had promised not to target passenger liners. Britain armed its merchant's ships, placing them beyond the protection of the cruiser rules, which demanded warning, and placing crews in a place of safety. The German U-boat campaigns were effective, sinking million tons of shipping between 1916 and January 1917.

The people of Ypres were brought in contact with First World War when ten thousand of German troops arrived on October 7, 1914. On October 13, the French and British armies arrived in the small Flemish market town in Western Belgium, just across from France. Ypres was described as being all the horrors of Somme and the bell of Verdun. Ypres knew war for the next four years, leaving almost every building razed to the ground. The arrival of the Americans in 1917 hastened the defeat of the Germans, and the last shell fell on the small town on October 14, that ended the Flanders Campaign on October 19, 1918. In the fight for Passchendaele and extra height areas northeast of Ypres, the Allies battled the hardship and pain of war, which never went well for them. The area was drenched with rain for a month. In the surrounding area around Ypres, over 1,700,000 soldiers of both sides were killed or wounded and an uncounted number of civilians were laid to rest. The German organization during the whole campaign was chaotic; the tactical and operation level ran completely contrast from the American's stability.

In 1917, Germany adopted a policy of unrestricted submarines warfare, realizing that America would eventually enter the war. Germany sought to strangle allied seas lines before the United States could transport troops overseas but could maintain only five long-range U-boats on stations. In February 1917, Germany had U-boats available in quantity, and in March, they made another effort to win the war and re-implement unrestricted submarine warfare against Britain and France. They sunk not only the allied but also neutral ships (United States) on sight. It was a large miscalculation, for, as a result; America declared war on Germany on April 6, 1917. President Woodrow Wilson had thought the Germans would be convinced to rescind the orders as in the 1915 case. But the Germans never flinched and concluded they could force the British and French to seek terms before the US Expeditionary Force could be established and brought to France. President Wilson broke off diplomatic relations with Germany, which was clear that war was possible.

The US Navy sent a battleship group to Scapa Flow to join with the British Grand Fleet, destroyer to Queenstown, Ireland and submarine to help guard convoys. Troopships were too fast for the submarines and never had to travel the North Atlantic in convoys. The merchant ships' beginning to travel in convoys, escorted on destroyers, made it difficult for the U-boats to find targets. U-boats had sunk more than 5,000 allied ships at a cost of 199 submarines. The 1917 events proved decisive in ending the war, although their efforts were not fully felt until 1918. The British naval blockade began to have a serious impact on Germany.

The *Northern Mine Barrage*: American and British crew laid a belt 230 miles long and mines 15 miles wide across the North

Sea, planting south and north from June to October 1918. The task was done with great execution and committed courage. For the convoy of thirteen USS ship crewmen, there was no time for relaxation, for the dangerous mission kept everyone alert, cruising the sea in fog and bad weather and doing a task never before done in the world.

For Russia, the war was devastating. Russia had patriotic rallying with Nicholas II. The growing influence of Gregory Rasputin over the Romanovs did a great deal to damage the royal family, and by the spring of 1917, the Romanovs, who had ruled Russia for just over three hundred years, were no longer in reign. Russia had been taken over by Kerensky and the Provisional Government. By the end of 1917, Russia was introduced to communist rule in areas of the Bolsheviks, led by revolutionary leader Vladimir Lenin. The transition of Russia over a space of four years would establish the world's first communist government. The devastation of World War I was the cause of the end of Romanovs' autocracy.

Allies gained control of Serbia and Greece when Bulgaria signed an armistice on September 29, 1918. Collapse of the Central Powers came swiftly. Germany had suffered six million casualties moved toward peace. Poor communications between the army's headquarters in Berlin and the frontline commanders did not help Molke keep control of the campaign or the planned defeat of France.

Prince Maximilian of Baden took charge of a new government as Chancellor of Germany to negotiate with the Allies. Telegraphic negotiations with President Wilson began immediately in the fervent hope that Wilson would offer better terms than the British and French. Instead, Wilson demanded the abdication of Kaiser.

With no resistance, the Social Democrat Philipp Scheidemann proclaimed the Republic on November 9, 1918. Imperial Germany was dead; a new Germany had been born: the second Chancellor of the Weimar Republic.

* Note: Italic paragraphs in diary section author included.

Defining Decision

T HIS BOOK DRAWS UPON the individual and collective experience of a young Texas boy born in 1894. It is crafted by a personal diary and keepsakes of a young boy's wisdom that came from seasons of despair and triumph. Walter Irvin's early years were spent on a farm near Bradshaw, Texas, that lay twenty-eight miles south of Abilene, twelve miles north of Winters, Texas, and one and a half miles north of the Runnels County line. Walter left Bradshaw for California as it was approaching the arrival of the Santa Fe Railroad. Bradshaw was named to honor landowner and donor C. M. Bradshaw who gave the railroad right-of-way.

Walter was one of ten children. He had six sisters and three brothers. An avid sports fan, Walter was active in sports while going to school and would work in the cotton fields for money. Walter would know hard times at an early age. He was from an unsettled abusive home environment. At the hands of their father, the children would know that abuse all too well. In 1911, on a trip to town to sell cattle, his father met his fate during a hotel fire. It was believed that his death was related with the money he had received from the sale of cattle.

At the tender age of fifteen, Walter, in a defining decision, struck out for California. Walter already knew an unusual life against poverty. Walter's difficult life seemed to have guided him away from home in search of a better life. His mother, knowing his difficult, stormy life, wanted better for her son and signed for him to enlist in the military. Walter was one of adventure with many interests. He enjoyed writing poetry, writing screen plays, and sketching cartoons; he also developed a strong interest in medicine during his early years in navy. Walter's difficult life seemed to guide him toward thinking for himself. A person's strength is his personality. To be courageous is to be guided by your own moral internal compass . . . Walter, the courageous young boy, went away from all that he had ever known with the hope of fulfilling his young dreams one day. His own diary, kept during his years in navy, tells much of his life's dreams as *only* Walter could tell in his own pin. In reading his diary, one may find himself or herself captivated as to how he seemed to have linked to a purpose and in the end fulfilled those dreams that he clung desperately to full shot. He was gifted with an aspiring mind–a person with *potential to be*.

There are pictures that show Walter may have served during the 1910 Mexican Revolutionary War with Mexico. General John "Jack" Mosby led the United States during the "Battle of Tijuana" from 1910 to June 22, 1911. The 1910 war featured a start of several in Mexican history. There was war each year until Mexico's President Obregón Álvaro was elected in 1920. Other than for pictures, there was no mention of his time that he served in the army or any mentioning of basic training until at the end of his diary, when he mentions about the *Navy Training Ship* in small details. He never kept a diary for World War II, but there are pictures, navy rating patches, and hat and discharge papers.

On January 18, 1913, Walter joined the navy. He served *sailing with the fair winds* mostly on the *USS Saranac*, a converted steamer assigned to *Mine Force One* in 1918; the two bases for the fleet was Inverness and Invergordon. He had a few transfer assignments with the *USS Princeton* and at the end of war was assigned with *USS Nanshan* (collier-home), *USS Hopkins* (patrol duty), and *USS Kilty* (destroyer), and was then transferred in and out of *USS Worden* (destroyer), *USS Chandler* (destroyer), and *USS Stewart* (destroyer).

Much had happened since Walter reenlisted; much had happened over the course of time. World War I was time like none other before—a place where airplanes, submarines, poison gas, and trucks were seen everywhere, and where artillery barrages and machine guns played a pivotal role in decimation of combatants.

Enlist in the United States Navy

W ALTER WROTE THE FOLLOWING in the back of his diary:

On January 17, 1913, I decided to enlist in the United States Navy and left home on January 18 at 7:00 p.m. by train, arrived in Abilene, Texas, ate supper at the Palace Hotel, and called up the *Gazette Newspaper*. The train left at 10:00 p.m. for Fort Worth and arrived in Fort Worth this a.m., I ate breakfast in the restaurant. I called the recruiting office and was unanimously passed and was given my ticket to Dallas. One hour later, I was in Dallas and then went to the General Office in the Post Office building. I passed an exam like a mentor, was given my meal ticket for five days, and boarded at Sue Lane's. I have been wandering around the city for four days and sent my clothes home this morning. I will leave for San Francisco tonight (Thursday), January 25. We're all aboard at 6:00 p.m., have first class passage, bunk and so on.

Spent a restless night–passed through the best of Texas in the dark. On Friday, I arrived in San Antonio this a.m., ate breakfast in depot restaurant, and did not have time to see any of the city.

Stopped two hours in El Paso, but things were in an undecided completion, and we were afraid to go far from the station. Saw a regiment of soldiers along the border. Continue to pass soldiers. Some fine farming country around El Paso. Country dry and hilly, alkali desert looking inhabited. I saw a few lonely squatters' shacks. Scenery poor, passed a lake far in the distance (forgotten the name). Arrived in San Francisco Saturday morning (scenery very pretty around Los Angles), passed in double file along streets muddy and dirty to United States Navy tug boat pier.

In due time, the tug arrives and conveys us to USNTS (*United States Navy Training Ship)* at Mare Island Navy Yard, Vallejo, California. A picturesque island indeed! Reported aboard the receiving ship *USS Intrepid* and ordered to the Rookie shack. We were hustled away before we were inside. Almost drawn to the barracks, we passed in single file. We're being fitted out with clothes, mattresses, and all of a sailor's exquisite as to marking clothes. Back at the shack, we scurried like a bunch of scared and confused rabbits, for some of the boys had been reprimanded upon their unmanly military ways of walking. And all the remainder was in a worse condition than the individuals who had been reprimanded. We're put to work on cloth-marking and so on; this finished, we were made to take a bath in salt water . . . it is January, remember! There was not a steam heater in a mile from there. You can imagine the pleasure we derived from the bath.

Attired in sailor's garb, we loaded our bag and hammock on our back, which weighed about 110 pounds, and proceeded to climb a hill with an inclination toward heaven of about 360 degrees. Darned Jimmy Leg would not let us rest, and we were afraid at the time to defy his authority; however, if I ever met him again, God help him! We were all about on arrival at the detention camp. No time to breathe, we were hustled down to the old marine barracks with our packs to get cots to sleep on. Upon returning, we deposited our baggage in designated shacks and were instructed in the manly art of rolling clothes. One little cuss offered to help me, who knew about as much of it as me, because I received a nice little lecture the next morning on the crummy condition of my bag. I said, "Nice," but the language was hardly appropriate for a Messiah. The old guy marine had been all over the world and knew about thirty languages, and so I got a nice lecture in each of the specific characters.

The following three weeks were torture. I tried to escape and even after an unusual hard reprimand, but luck was against me–or with me–I should say, for I failed in the attempt. At last, the three weeks of hell were terminated by my passing the required exam for promotion to the company. Then I tried for drilling in parade at barracks, so one month of life was much better; I passed it, but when I fell ill with mumps, I was in the hospital for three weeks; this period of time decided my future naval career. I went back to the barracks and made application for a change in rating. I passed the required exam–rate changed on April 16, 1913–and worked as a Pharmacist Mate. Returned to hospital, was put in charge of mumps ward, then three more weeks quarantine in measles ward doing medical staff work–first aid, nursing and so on. Promoted to surgical ward "R" (Recovery) duty, *here* lasted four days, then orders arrived for transfer to Samoa on June 2, 1913. Made preparations in double quick time and boarded the *USS Sonoma* (mail carrier) which was bound for Pago Pago port and naval station. It was the largest ship on the Pacific. Passed Honolulu, had eight hours' liberty, which we spent to the best advantage possible. Saw several of the old historical buildings. Left

Honolulu for final destination, weather continued fair. Arrived at Pago Pago (capital of American Samoa, on the southern coast of Tutuila, Inland) after a thirteen-day voyage and fell sick for three days out from San Francisco. At the United States Navy Station, I was ordered for duty at Tutuila Hospital, where my long list of experience valued inestimable to me—it began and has continued up to the present time of writing.

Walter wrote

Notice, important: when good sailors die, their soul goes to heaven. When bad sailors die, their soul is donated to a disastrous voyage of wandering and terminating at last in the hell of all hells—Samoa.

January 9, 1914, Tutuila, Pago Pago; American Samoa: I purchased a diary today, determined to keep diary for the rest of my time while serving in the navy. Heard today that I will be shifted to the Naval Dispensary on Monday but undecided as to whether I want to make a change or not. Shipmate Leinquest is anxious for a change; I don't think he will like it after he has been here awhile, and am curious to know the outcome.

January 10: United States Naval Station Pago Pago. I got up this morning, feeling fine and dandy. Played ball, and in the afternoon, with the ship, my team won with a score 4-10. There was nothing else of importance—it did not rain today.

The Samoan or Samoa Islands is an archipelago of thirteen islands, covering 1,170 square miles in the Central South Pacific.

Due to colonialism, the Samoa Islands and people were divided by western powers. It was also referred to by early European explorers as the Navigators' Island–Pago Pago Harbor, an eroded volcanic crater that cuts deeply into the south coast. The terrain is mostly heavily eroded mountains with a flat coastal plain on the south coast. Official language(s): English and Samoan. Motto: Samoa, Muamua Le Alua; "Samoa, Let God be First."

Walter Irvin after he left West Texas and went to California.

Bradshaw, Texas.

Bradshaw high school basketball team.

General Mosby on way to Surrender 1911.

W. (William) C. Morris.

L-R: Walter Irvin and friend.

USN Training Station San Francisco.

Station Band

S. S. Sonoma on July 13, 1913, Walter sent card to sister Vivian,
that said: A picture of the mail steamer which I came
over on–the largest ship on the Pacific W.

Looking toward entrance of Pago Pago Harbor.

United States Naval Station
Pago Pago

JANUARY 11, 1914, I made my first suppository today–learned what it was after almost killing a woman with what I supposed was to be the correct drug.

I have made a date with Miss Anderson to go with her to the top of Matafao Mountain in the near future. Miss Anderson said that she supposed she would have to let Miss Humphrey go too.

Heard today that the ship is going to Sidney soon, and I am anxious to know whether I am going to get to go or not. Tomorrow I go to the other hospital for duty. It has not rained today.

I found the poem today that I have been trying to write ever since I have been in the navy.

Tuesday, January 12: Came down today to this place of duty and found it to be far from what Toots has it cracked up to be. I got the dispensary operating room and ward to oversee. Nothing else of importance happened. Oh yes, I blistered my hands helping to fix up the basketball court.

January 13: Nothing much doing today. I put up several prescriptions on Wednesday. I have decided I like this place better than the other hospital.

January 14: Nothing much happening this morning. The next two days, I played ball in the afternoon with my team winning another game of two to one.

January 15: Today was the big day in making preparations for fumigating freight and mail, and then this evening played basketball.

January 16: The steamer arrived this morning at 10:00 a.m. Toots and I went aboard the altar (where religious ceremonies are performed) about 2:00 p.m. for fumigating and did not return until after dark and missed our supper. Four of the best men on the station left today. Sure hate to see Sowell, Ammon, Williams, Duffy, and Croft go.

Saturday 17: Had to get up at four o'clock this morning to release the mail from quarantine. Toots and Steward got the dickens from Dr. Ely this Saturday for not taking better care of the mail.

Played ball this afternoon, my team winning another victory with a score 11-12; it was a rotten game! I played center field on account of having a sore hip and a sore toe. Blackie got very goatee because I ran over him going to home plate.

On February 14, 1914, the American Samoan Nurses Training School was opened in Fagatogo, next to the hospital, under the director of acting Chief Nurse Mary H. Humphreys and Nurse Corinne Anderson of the US Navy's Female Nurse Corps. The first three that studied nursing were Initi'a, Fe'iloia, and Pepe, who were graduates of the London Missionary. On January 19, 1914, the Department of

Public Health was established in America Samoa and was headed by the Senior Medical Officer of the United States Navy Station Tutuila.

September 2, 1914: Nothing of importance happened today … laid around all afternoon. I couldn't get a ball game scheduled. The governor has a feast in Pago Pago.

(Samoan: 'Pago 'Pago) The historical capital of Pago Pago is the seat of government at Fagatogo and the office of the governor is in Utulei. Tutuila became American Samoa as the result of a hurricane, and during that period of annexing, Germany got Upolu and Savaii, Britain got Fugi, and the United States got Tutuila. Tutuila being rocky and mountainous with the Pago Pago harbor was ideal and so became United States Navy property. Pago Pago was a coaling and repair station for the United States Navy. At the start of World War I in 1914, New Zealand, an independent country of Samoa, sent two destroyers over and kicked the Germans out of their islands.

I think they will start pumps on the Princeton tomorrow.

I will be boxing four rounds as usual tonight. Time has passed very fast, many things has happened since I last wrote in this little book. The *USS Princeton* went under water.

On July 11, 1914, while the Princeton was patrolling off the coast of Samoa, it struck an uncharted rock during a violent storm. A hole was punched in her hull, and the ship took on considerable flooding that placed it in a dangerous situation. The Princeton *began to go down by the bow and the forward gun deck to awash. Acting quickly, her crew was able to get her under way and steam back to the Naval Station, Tutuila, and Samoa. The captain of the* Princeton *received a letter from the secretary of the navy of the department's commendation for the coolness and bravery shown by the ship's company when the* USS Princeton *struck an uncharted rock.*

War is going on over in Europe. I passed my exam and everything. Sure wished I had kept my book up-to-date. I am sure going to from now on. I am back at Samoan Hospital; things are going fine. Toots and I went four rounds tonight and, if anything, he will put it over me tonight. I will be going to bed pretty soon if nothing turns up.

Well, something turned up all right! They started pumps on the *Princeton* this morning. Canvas putting wear on smokestack carrier and had to abandon work today. War is going on over in Europe. Today, Turkey declared war on Bulgaria; otherwise, nothing out of the usual in the hospital. Had two operations.

September 4: Today was streamer day to be fumigated as usual. The hookers from the governor's house went home. The woman, Mrs. Gensen, went home also. They started pumps on the *Pagonis* and discovered another hole.

Apia was taken by English on August 10. *Apia is the capital of Samoa and the second largest island in Western Samoa.*

Alofa came back today, and Knight left on today's streamer. Koheer and Marburg left for Academy.

September 5: Glick walked today—I did not! I am *anything* this week. Got working on the *Princeton* today. No wireless (radiotelegraph). Toots, David Dan, Red, Skinny, and the rest of the bunch went to Leone today. Everything about was as usual in the hospital, I am studying up on anesthetics.

September 6: Everything was about as usual. One kid croaked with Feolun, it was my first experience with the disease. Toots came back from Leona. Old Lanham refused to go back to duty. I have been reading up on the war. Today, I received papers from Sydney Friday.

September 7: Think I examined about two hundred stools today; all I can see tonight is feces. Found one new organism—to me—the lamblia intestinalis.

Moved into our new house today. I am trying to study by a darned old lantern tonight. We have to take an examination in general education Saturday, new orders from the department. The Germans have abandoned their plans of taking Paris at present. Loaned Fatilua one dollar today, which is to be paid payday next.

September 8: Heard today we have to take an examination in general education every week. Studied upon a few subjects this p.m. Skinny and the bunch came up to see me tonight. Studying upon the hookworm today, fished some out of a fresh stool.

September 9: Things are going fine today—still at my lab work. No ball game, everyone has gone on a strike. They are going to start rehearsals tonight on the minstrel show. I am trying to figure out a plot for a movie. Another dance at the governor's house tonight—may go down for a spell by-and-by.

September 10: Had an operation. I assisted for the first time alone. Big fall operation. Irwin and Mac had a little misunderstanding today over some stories. I went down to the other place to see Dan about a play we composed some time ago. I have another plot afoot tonight to type yet. I have to go down and fumigate the SOF (Special Operations Forces) Combatant Craft Systems in the morning at five.

September 11: Everything is just about as usual today. Got my stain (character blemish) from Erwin today. Am still planning that movie tonight.

September 12: Saturday—it rained like heck all day and is still raining. Germany retreated all around today. I am off tomorrow. Have two movies underway tonight that I will finish tomorrow.

September 13: It rained like the mischief today. Streamers arrived at 6:15. I went aboard for the first time and was introduced to Mr. Plnax, nephew to Secretary of State. He is going to take a Samoan villager to the fair. Governor's secretary came as well. Word was Dr. Pretief would be down near the boat, also Dan's. No mail tonight.

United States Naval Station Tutuila, Samoa, September 14, 1914: Arose early this morning and walked down to the post office and got my mail. It has almost quit raining at last. Two of the boys were put in the brig last night for interference. Toots has gone down to rehearse tonight. Studying my lessons. I have stopped the movies for present. Red is going home in the next boat.

September 15: I cut out the movies for my studies and started on an ancient history today. They started pumps on the *Princeton* this afternoon.

September 16: The old *Princeton* is afloat at last. They have her alongside the customer's warehouse. Everybody is cussing the MCM (Mine Squadron-Counter Measure work), reported Irwin this a.m.

September 17: I compiled my history of Egypt last night and will study *Babylonia* (Ancient Empire of Mesopotamia in the Euphrates River Valley) and *Assyria* (Ancient Empire and Civilization of West Asia in the upper valley of the Tigris River—ancient name for the northeastern part of modern Iraq) tonight. It has been raining like heck for the last three days of study.

October 6: There has been so dang much happening the last few weeks. I haven't had time to do anything. Woodruff's court-martial has been sure in. The governor went home in the last boat with his wife. I can't write any reason for his leaving. Dr.

Ely and Dr. P. Red went home, and the photographer also left us. Miss Kennedy, who the paymaster was after, also beat it.

The *USS Princeton* is well on the way to recovery. She is red-leaded and almost ready for her trial trip.

Old Bill and the Princess were married on September 30; they were given a hell of a chivalry also. There was hell popping on the mess this month. Old Speedy run the assessment up to $6.00 this month, and the Chief Petty Officers raised a hell of a stink this month. They are going to start their own mess in Tulifite barracks tomorrow.

Doctor Ely's wife and children, Chester, Catherine, and baby left for Berkley, California the first of October. We presented her an ostrich plume. She gave us a supper the night before she left. I worked most of the day in the laboratory today and for a while out on the grounds for exercise.

October 7: Could not get a ball game—all the boys were working. I got to scare up $1,500 within the next week. Tried for some stamp swapping today; however, I never made out. Mess is doing very well now since the Chief Petty Officers left.

October 16: Everything as usual—four new doctors arrived on the last steamer. One seems to be a pretty good fellow. Loaned Paleaie $2.88 this month, David $2.00, and Willie $2.00. Lemquist and I change details tomorrow. Dr. Parham is going home in the next steamer. Dan is leaving. Their "tefoga" was called off a day or two ago. New order 110 arrived on the last boat. I am going to write to Joe this steamer and ask him his opinion of my buying my own books and starting in at a medical course of four years. I can get transportation and everything to San Francisco. I am undecided as to my next step.

Loaned Fatilua $1.50 today. Willie paid me the $2.00 he borrowed.

November 2: David paid me $2.00 and still owes me a dollar. Bofu borrowed $2.00; Paleaie paid me on the 28.

Dr. Parham left in the last steamer in the day along with Daniels, Skinny, Mrs. Wenter, Lient, Beall and family, and the commander and his wife. I gave Dr. Parham a big smoke before he left.

We have $150.00 to build a baseball diamond. We started work on October 27 and have finished more than one-third. I will have only fifty-nine dollars from this month.

I wrote Joe this last mail and also sent a letter to the Medical University of Texas, asking them for catalog and so on. I have started smoking cigarettes again. Some talk of a field meet for Thanksgiving Day. We expect to start playing ball again in a couple of weeks. One of the new doctors is a baseball fan, so Toots and I won't have any trouble getting off on ball day.

November 1914: Willie, Fatilua, David, Toots, Darland, and Paleaie all paid up. Everything is going quite fair the last few weeks. Dr. Parker came down to relieve Dr. Ely. He performed one operation since he came.

Irwin and "I" had a scrape here a few days ago—seem to be friendly terms now. I was put on the committee to get the sports for Thanksgiving, but there will be none. Had a baseball game Saturday, have the grounds in pretty good shape now. We will have a game on Thursday. Dr. Ely and Dr. Hayward go on a *Malaga "606" Campaign* today.

December 1: Tomorrow is the *ghast* (ghost like) *walk*. I won't draw anything this month. Have about thirty dollars standing out, which are enough for two more months. Played a couple of games since I wrote last—my team won the first by a score of six to one, and the ships' team won the last with a score three to zero. Will play again tomorrow, expecting to win. The last game we lost. Toots pitched, and I caught—it was his first game. We could not expect much from him. Old Speedy was in charge up here the last week—had the old boy a little worried at times over some of the diagnostic case reports. The rumor is that there will be a change before long in the hospital, compliment at this station.

December 3: Collected all my money today. Loaned Willie $5.00 and Tatilua $5.50. Big blow-out in honor of Dr. Ely tonight—he leaves Sunday.

December 6: Two boys, Kholi and Warlburg, fell down in their entrance examinations for academy, both deserted afterward.

Steamer Day: Received a few letters from home today, everything is all OK. Received my catalog from Texas A&M College, have decided to start school when I get back and get a little preliminary education before I try to study medicine. If I can work with my buddy in Oakland, I will start to school there—did not hear from this fast as I expected to.

Saw champions of World Swimmers swim yesterday. The Duke of Honolulu sure can wave. Seven new men came down this boat. Dr. Ely left. He gave a very nice office toast good-bye. The new senior medical officer's wife is sure a rounder.

December 8: Carpenter and I went out to the Tagalog Falls this morning and had a very good time. Old Wesley received his tuba today. Lt. Charles Armijo Woodruff is the acting governor now. Paymaster Jenter and Pay Clerk Abbot and his wife left yesterday. Heard from Dan yesterday; he is in one hell of a scrape with another girl.

December 9-11: Have been working on my lessons again—don't know how long I will keep it up. Arithmetic is my lesson for this week. Hell since the new governor started work. The lift was pried up yesterday on the prohibition wagon. Everybody's stewed to the gills at supper this evening. Did not play ball today for the opening of Solf killed everything. Dance also tonight.

December 10-11: Pago Pago, Samoa Hospital: Everything about as usual, I played ball last Saturday. Tuesday assisted Dr. Parker and Dr. Hayward in a hydrocele operation. It took one hour and ten minutes to perform the operation. Dr. Hathaway is away at Malaga (a city of South Spain northeast of Gibraltar), expect him back before long. Things look like war with Mexico from what we hear from the wireless. I hope to get away from here before they start; otherwise, chances for relief are very small. There is quite a bunch going home on the next boat.

Day after Christmas: Well, my second and hope, my last Christmas I spent yesterday. Miss Anderson and Miss Humphrey gave a Christmas for a bunch of the little half-caste heathens (one who adheres to a religion other than Judaism, Christianity, or Islam), Toots and I bought them a Japanese hand-embroidered silk Kimono a piece, only cost twenty-two dollars. I acted like Santa Claus, had quite a number of distinguished guests. I had a good dinner at mess. Most of the booze has been consumed in the last twenty-four hours than I ever imagined possible.

Had the dickens of an earthquake the other night, I have felt several but this outclassed them all—the good ship Olf (Outlaying Field) has all ports open.

December 30, 1914: Christmas days have passed on *unaware* and just one day left of 1914. Every one of us is convalescing. Seems every man on the ship had a fight with his best friend.

Big tall Collins the Yeoman (clerical duties) and little ordinary seaman, Paul, loom above all the others. The rug fights and other trashing of importance have happened with the exception of the ball games. I got spiked in the ankle by one of the very Yeoman today. He and I have grievance to square off in the next game.

Paymaster McCarty and Lient Davis called a meeting Monday of all baseball players. Slide and Blackie picked all the best men off the ship and station divided them equally. We had our first game today. Blackie, as usual, got goatish and played hell with the game. We lost the game with a score of six to seven.

Note: Damnedest hottest day I have seen in Samoa. The temperature registered 115 degrees in the shade. At present, things are not as hot as they perhaps could be, but you can still smell sulfur and brimstone holes still cover the earth. Two big operations on for tomorrow, so got to get up at five to start sterilizers and so on; will go to bed early tonight.

Assisted doctors, Parker and Hathaway, in two operations today—no trouble, everything moved smoothly.

Today, the *eagle screamed* (payday). Willie paid me the $5.00, and Talilua paid me $5.00 and owes me .50. My bills were $28.00 this month; I am sending Vivian my $20.00 for motion picture course this month.

January 1, 1915: I spent a very quiet New Year. I had nothing to do this morning. This afternoon, I went across the Vitia Pass for a climb. Dam near, choked for water but finally discovered a little food in the side of the pack.

Governor gave an entertainment party at the mansion, but I did not attend. The *dawn* came in yesterday morning laden with bad booze, so all the sailors proceeded to get inebriated. A number of fights ensued this evening. Well, I am wondering where I will spend the next few years. Don't expect to spend another in Samoa. Hooray, the mail comes tomorrow! I received two letters this mail—one from Dr. Fuller and one from Possum. No newcomers, no governor. Heard the tug *Fortune* would be down to relieve the *Princeton* on 20 January. War is progressing weekly. Toots and Lanham were shifted this month. I suppose Lanham and I will get along OK.

January 19, 1915: Played ball Saturday, we won, had a rather rotten game of six to eight. Executive officer has issued an order that all men report for practice once a week and for a game twice a week.

Hell has been popping today, last night; a Fijian tried to assault the woman prisoner. The man was tried this morning and sentenced to ten years in prison. Damn, nearly had a war! All the Fijian guards marched to the governor's office and demanded that chief MCM be relieved from duty. Governor Woodruff told them to go to hell and get out of his office. They threatened. He warned them that if they started any trouble, he would wire the fleet and blow up the whole damned island. All ammunition was removed from the barracks—imagine, this evening all were ordered to bear arms tonight. Everything seems to be fairly quite at present. They are having a big meeting in Fagaloa tonight to determine their future course. Aleck Forsyth, the former governor's interpreter, was tried in court and found guilty of scandal and such stuff and sentenced to be departed by the first available steamer. Hoping we have war—I retire!

January 28: The war did not come but the governor gave Aleck Forsyth another trial—trial is not terminated yet. Kelland was investigated in the meantime. Several prostitutes abducted in the last few days. Two boys came in the other night with gunshot wounds. Was up all night! One died last night. Orders from the doctor were not to let the other boy leave the hospital, but if he did, they'd take him home through apprehended orders but won't do it again. The other boy slipped out, Lanham has returned from a fifteen mile hike after him. Quite a merry jocose episode!

Sure do have *my fun* with Lanham and Pepe. He is dead struck on her and her about him in return for his warm affections. Now just imagine the results—me teasing them.

Miss Anderson almost got in governor's trial a day or two prior to the first happening. I am going to put in my application for transfer tomorrow. By the way, I finished Roosevelt's *African Game Trails* a few days ago, also, *The Duchess of Few Clothes* and *From Log Cabin to White House*. Sure enjoyed the latter and profited by it also, now I have started reading *Lives of Our President* today.

Say—darn near forgot to mention I just quit smoking cigarettes a week ago. Sure feel better. Intellectual powers are in much better condition than they have been for some time.

Lanham has walked in with ring off.

January 29, 1915: I put in my application for transfer today, I have not heard back from it yet. I am hoping and praying the doctor and governor approves it. Mail day passed, received a few presents from some of my kin. Received new chairs and a few other things for club soda fountain and so on. Arrived for our store on this boat. Have changed the mess hall again—thank God! Jimmy is cooking, happy went to butcher shop, Pepe and Dip Lanham are getting along fine.

I mastered *square root* today, the *George Washington Administration, John Adams,* and *Thomas Jefferson* too. I have resolved to study all I can while at this place. Guy has made a crop or two for mama. Finished my correspondence course, to teach school the subsequent year is my finale resolution.

February 5: Reading and studying alternately the past three days in Arithmetic rates and fractions. *Lewis of Our Presidents*, by Alfred Henry Lewis, and also, *The Hills* and *Hampshire, Dad, Grammar–Etymology*. The ship has been to Leone twice and is now on her way to Manua with supplies. Skinny returned from Ventura, California on Sunday and stated that he left my friend Daniels drunk in a cabaret show. Poor old Dan is an example of years in the United States Navy.

I caught a phenomenal glimpse into Miss Mary Humphrey's character today. The old lady certainly has some philosophical foresight as far as physiognomy is concerned and is really appalling. Tomorrow is Sunday. Puzzled as to what I would be doing if I were back in my home environment tonight.

Princeton arrived from Manua this evening and everything is blown to hell over there–the worst storm ever recorded. Government will be compelled to support them for the next five years. Saw some of the photos. Lucky made it to Manua today, which sure is torn up. Wyandotte arrived from Brisbane, Australia today and will leave for San Francisco tomorrow. Has coal for Australia.

USS Wyandotte left this a.m. Dave and I came down to Viatoga today through Honolulu. The Honolulu cricket game is in progress there. Heard before we left that Aleck Forsyth had disappeared and the governor has a $100.00 reward for his capture.

Arrived on Valentine's Day about 6:00 p.m., not a darn girl to be found their all over at Honolulu. Joe decided to pursue a rather bold plan this Nuir Gourg to play the Fomai Strut. It seemed to work fairly well.

Left the village this morning about 9:00; did not get to see the shark and turtle. I have two operations next week. Well, I must turn to my studies. Read Morgan's *Life of Lincoln* the other day and sure liked it fine. In my estimation, he was a more intelligent man than Garfield. It put a decided change in my mind about the civil war. Read the *Daughter of Anderson Craw* last week but did not consider its comedy extra appealing. Would decidedly prefer the quaint comedy of *The Hills of Hampshire* that I previously read.

Monday: Four operations today, everything passed as smooth as could be expected. I assisted Dr. Parker and Humphrey.

Found Aleck Forsyth on Tuesday; he is in Pago Pago. District Governor Maugas Fale will deport him tomorrow via open boat. Almost had a scrape last night, for Aleck did not want to go. Officers from the ship and ten armed men were sent. Things looked pretty lively for a while–peace was at last restored through the diplomatic prudence of District Governor Mangas.

Wednesday: Aleck left this a.m. at seven for Apia (capital of Samoa), accompanied by squad of armed police. Mitchell and Wilson trials were thrown out of court on lack of evidence.

Thursday: Our dear little yard foreman J. W. Jewett was soaring among the clouds of joy and bliss today; he drank a little too much of the red man's fire water and was quietly overcome with joy.

Friday: Nothing of importance happened today. Everything passed smoothly enough. Miss Humphrey sent us a swell pumpkin pie today. I made short work of the set element.

Saturday: Everything went smoothly this a.m. Played ball this afternoon with the Fite-Fite guards. I pitched a no-hit game and credited with twenty strikeouts. Beat my record against them and every other man who previously pitched against them for they were surely a bunch of batters. It revives my interest in baseball for I have been declining for the last four months. I am writing a complete record of my time in the navy–that is, all I can remember since my enlistment.

Sunday, twelve midnight: Expect to spend a sleepless night. A heck of a storm is on the way Sunday. Barometer has dropped 19 degrees since 8:00 a.m. As I write, I can feel the breath of a monster only felt in Samoa. Will adjourn to tying houses to "terra firma" (dry ground)–by God, it rained OK, and I had to work in the whole damn thing.

Moved all the patients from number *two* to number *one* in the teeth of the climax of the storm and had everything on number 1 strapped down when a puff of wind stronger than atlas shivered it like an egg. It was the hardest storm we have had in sometime. Thought the whole damn thing was going to be a repetition of Manua. A coconut limb missed my bean by the fraction of an inch. I have been praying since. Old Lanham and I got some strange nipping last night.

February 25: Slide was up last night and got pretty well inebriated as usual. Read a book last night that put new thoughts into my head called the "answer" for adults. Started me thinking in a different line and studied some over it too. I have started reading *The Eyes of the World* this afternoon by Harold Bell Wright–borrowed them from Miss Humphrey. Tomorrow the *eagle screams*–drawing nothing tomorrow.

February 26: I drew only thirty dollars, have over fifteen loaned out. Hast walked (AWOL) today and Aleck Forsyth returned. They would not let him land in Apia. I read Harold Bell Wright's book *The Eyes of the World* and in my opinion, it is his masterpiece.

Impresses me favorably indeed, he sure has a perfected mode of picturing scenery mentally.

CPO (Chief Petty Officer) mess hall is giving Jim Flynn his farewell supper tonight. Hope there is not a Judas in the merry party.

Saturday, February 27: Tomorrow is steamer day. I don't expect to get any mail this trip. I haven't written home for some time. Nothing unusual happened today. Got a little ball practice this evening after supper and started reading a book entitled *Science and Health and Key to the Scripture*–interesting to read, it gives a person a view of both sides.

February 28: Still reading book mentioned. Nothing happened. Steamer won't be in before tomorrow.

Monday, March 1: Steamer arrived at 6:00 a.m., two new nurses aboard, one Hospital Apprentice First Class (HA1c) and wife of new governor arrived on Hospital Ship. Saw old Jim Corbitt aboard the steamer. Flynn is going on this steamer. Have plans for a cleanup in Sydney if things turn out OK. I received a short letter from Vivian (sister) today.

Tuesday: Completed *The Inside of the Cup* by Winston Churchill–it left me with a profound impression regarding religion. Saw one of the nurses today–hardly knew what to think of her. I am going to get a picture of the entire Samoa Hospital Corps made next week–if possible. Went to the movie picture show this evening and spent a quiet day. I came near having a serious argument with the steward over some eye remedies. McCarty and Mitchell leave in eight weeks.

Thursday: The new stewards came up for duty.

Friday: Miss Smiling, the new nurse, took charge of the operating room. It relieves me of considerable responsibility.

Heard today the men that arrived on Sunday will be signed for duty in the new dispensaries at Manua and Leone . . . I don't envy them. God knows this is far enough away for me to live. Carpenter will have finished drug store by the end of the week. Next, I am in a sanguine frame of mind toward that position. Ship leaves for Manua next Monday morning at six o'clock sharp. Toots and Irvin are going also.

USS Princeton in 1903.

USS Princeton: taken from stern while submerged
on July 11, 1914 when ship hit a reef.

USS Princeton: seen from Customs Dock.

Galley used by *Princeton* after July disaster.

USS Princeton after resurrection.

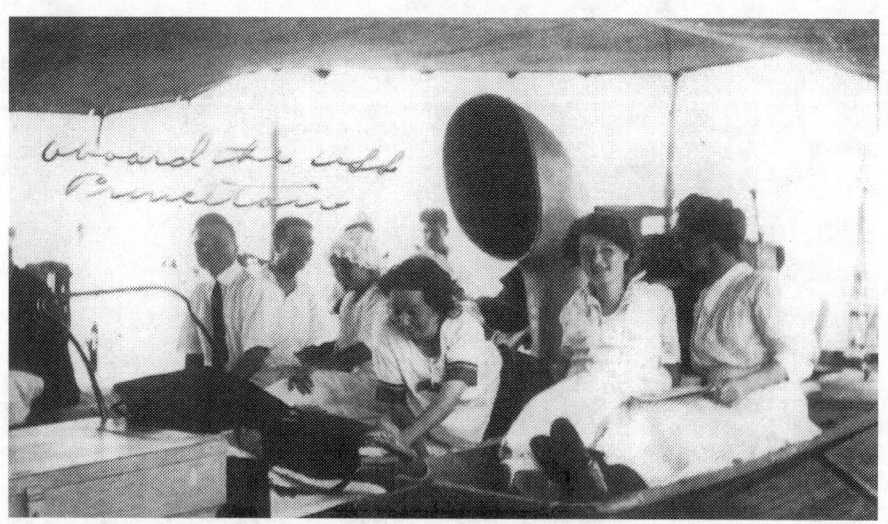

A load of sick people *en route* for Apia aboard the *USS Princeton*.

Surgeon E. W. Parker after the February storm.

What was left of a brick and stone church after storm.

Picture of officers, missionaries and a few others: 1. Judge
Stronach; 2. Missionary Hough; 3. Mrs. C. C. D. Stearns;
4. Governor C. D. Stearns; 5. Surgeon C. F. Ely; 6. Zient
Woodruff; 7. Chied Machinst, Battenger; 8. Assistant Surgeon,
Parham; 9. Mrs. Parham; 10. Civil Engineer, Pratt 11–12–13–14
and 15. Professor of Mathematics–Updegraff is Professor at
Annapolis School for officers–merely on detached duty–Samoa;
men with stripes on shoulder are officers of USN.

Tutuila, American Samoa.

Samoan Hospital: here is the crowd that usually gathers every
morning for dressings etc. Surgeon C. F. Ely seated at table.

Picture L-R: Ward 2 Operating room; Ward 2 Administration Building; Ward 3 training school for native girls. These buildings are a great deal larger than they appear to be.

Working with Pumps on the *USS Saranac*.

Crewman taking five.

5th and 6th Divisions of *USS Saranac*. Walter Irvin at right on
fourth row–cap is tilted to left.

Some of the *Saranac's* crewmen.

Flag Day or New Governor

B Y THE WAY, NEW Governor John Martin Poyer was inaugurated on Thursday. I am expecting a wireless when the steamer goes up from Sydney. Flynn is on the alert if everything turns out as expected. Slide and I will purchase our discharge in the near future. The new nurse has settled for good. The *Princeton* left for Manua at 4:00 p.m. this day with Lemquist and Irvin accompanying her. Expect her to go home in September. Glick and Slide were up last evening. Proceeded and got Jeff to borrow $10.00 from Miss Humphrey to buy a Kava bowl yesterday. We had our pictures taken yesterday. Quite a funny little thing happened in the meantime. Haven't been feeling very well today. Will retire early.

March 14-15, 1915: Steffenoy arrived from Apia today. Haven't heard the reason for his jealous journey . . . must have been urgent business. Had a little fire down at paymaster McCarty's house today. It was extinguished in an extraordinary comical manner. Sly returned from Manua. Mexico is again threatened with war. Chances are they will annihilate her this time. Have two operations next week.

Another Sunday passed quietly enough. General Glies was up to spend the morning with me. Banker is going to Leone next week for future duty. I don't envy his transfer in the least. Read a splendid little comedy titled *The Shorty McCabe*, a fascinating little comedy. Danny Webster chaperoned today; he seems to have made a hit with the duchess, Miss Smiling, the new nurse.

March 16: Two big operations today. Assisted Dr. Parker and Miss Humphreys—no trouble. Banker departed for Leone aboard the *Princeton*.

Anxious to have Friday roll around, for it may mean a change in my life's program. Operated on old lady Hough yesterday for appendicitis—this operation is just coming in style for people in this hole.

March 18: Payday yesterday, drew $10.00 and left $9.00 on books. Tomorrow is my day for a wireless.

March 20: Plenty of rain yesterday; tanks and reservoir filled and overflowing. No wireless arrived today. Sorely afraid changes were not as we expected. MCM informed me that I will get the drug store this p.m. and will install the fountain on Monday.

Tuesday, March 23: Everything as usual the past two days. *Princeton* made trial trip today; don't know how she breasted the waves. She is just entering the harbor. Read Robert G. Ingersoll's *Crimes against Criminals* today; he is a strange-minded writer in my opinion. Any man of ordinary intelligence could do nothing except Aquinas (*Aquinas' Moral, Political and Legal Philosophy*), with such straightforward and sound logic. To read in future Robert Ingersoll's *Some Mistakes of Moses*.

April 1: Pretty near neglected my diary the past week during all the excitement last Friday, the 25th. Hunt and I went to Leone's village twelve miles east of here on the southwest coast of Tutuila Island, American Samoa, South Pacific. Had a nice trip, enjoyed a good bath after our hard riding, and then partook of a delicious repast prepared by our host's wife. After supper, we paid our friend, Banker, a short visit. Dr. Parker came over in the meantime, and we had a quiet jocular chat. I retired early at twelve midnight, arose bright and early the next day, had breakfast, walked over, and assisted Banker with his clinic until twelve noon. Ate a fine dinner cooked and served by the benevolent Mrs. Banker. Then Hunt and I strolled out to look for girls. We knew it was against the rules to smoke in the school, but Hunt dared me to roll a cigarette. I told him I was game, so we proceeded. The old lady did not take notice at first but a whiff of smoke soared her way and she lit upon us with twelve claws. Lord, I never heard a woman come so near swearing. We had some fun over it when we reached a secluded spot–but not before!

Saturday night: Everyone enjoyed a show given by the native women alone titled *Joseph and His Brethren*. First show ever given by any of the natives alone was a puff in, laughed for a week. Lord, Saturday night had a native uprising. Would not have given one cent for my life the whole night, but the ship's company arrived in time to save the day. It started over a cricket game. Coming home, I ran into a bunch of them. "I don't know that they want any harm because when they let out that diabolical yell, I faded into the atmosphere–but I do know I nearly killed a horse."

Steamers arrived at 5:00 a.m. Got one letter from Layman. No news about the *Princeton* going home. Operated Monday, expect to hear from Flynn in the next steamer.

Murray is going on a thirty-days' leave tomorrow, and I will be detained in the dressing room until he returns. Went out to Ta' Qali Falls yesterday and had a fine dinner and a good time in general. *Princeton* went to Apia on Friday and returned on Sunday. Another mishap—she tried to hale (haul-pull) schooner off the reef, collided and smashed the stern, but had no permanent damage.

I have an operation duty tomorrow. I was up to see Tony, Jess, and Lin last evening. *Eagle screams* today. I am drawing twenty dollars, leaving eighteen on books.

April 15: Loaned David $5.00 plus $1.75, and Tatilua $6.00. I am trying to cut expenses this month; will make an allotment of $20.00 this coming month. Quite a storm blowing for the last month—*Princeton* has been putting off the trip to Manua for that account. Quite a program for 17th Flag Raising Day in Samoa.

April 19: Flag-raising sports were hardly as good as last year's, decided lack of preparation. Slide and I went out last evening; he lost forty dollars, and I won five—stayed up all night. Sleepy as the dickens this a.m. and as usual, more work to do. I loaned Paleaie eleven dollars today.

First Flag Raising Day in Samoa. Here the people are seen in their best Sunday clothes. The *USS Princeton* is firing salute in distance.

Tutuila Samoa Inauguration of new governor on March 1, 1915.

Governor's garden–Government Hill, Pago Pago, Samoa.

March 2, 1915, Samoan Hospital Martyrs Pago Pago, Tutuila, American Samoa. L-R: Viola Gass, Miss Anderson; Miss Snelling & Mary Humphrey. Front row L-R: Dip Lanhan, P. A., Surgeon G. S. Hathaway, and Walter Irvin, acting steward.

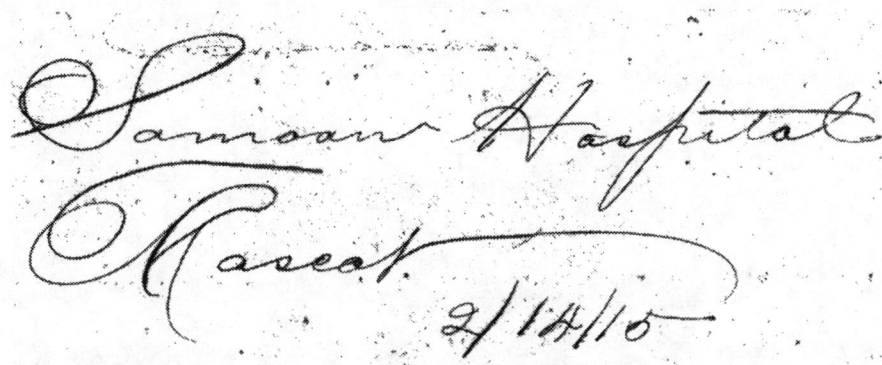

Samoan Hospital Mascot, February 14, 1915–some of Walter's writing.

Drawing of Walter Irvin.

Drawing of Walter Irvin.

April 20: *Princeton* arrived last evening from Manua, left old Sims over there without a house as usual. Lanham is raising the devil because Glick has gotten his job up here. He is going to the ship for duty. He did not want to leave his girl up here in care of me.

H. A. Steamer arrived this a.m. My application came back approved along with L. Irwin's and Lanham's. Miss Mary Humphrey left today, also Paymaster McCarty, Mitchell, Mrs. Parker, Miss McCarty, and Mary Parker. Things may be pretty loose over across the road now the old lady is gone. With the S.A., got one rate.

I think I will be going home in June. Received a letter from home, Mama—she wants to know where I am. Guy seems to be boosting them up a little.

We are supposed to receive a shipment of baseballs on this shipment.

April 27: Operated today, old G. S. Hathaway went through three bells and a jingle in eleven minutes. Had quite a good time; Miss Anderson invited us over for a dance last evening. They purchased Dr. Parker's graph phone last night. I may go down to the movies this evening.

April 28: Rather a busy day with three operations. Practiced baseball this afternoon; damned old sky pilot knocked us out of a nice evening. Glick is over there now. I am waiting the signal to come—seems as though it is a long time. Saw my orders for transfer today. Woody called me into the office as I was passing.

May 1: Had quite a nice time over across the way last evening, almost learned to dance; met a charming little woman also. Went to dinner yesterday evening; did not expect to see them this evening but tomorrow. Oh, I'm working like the dickens at present. Standing every evening on watch–Murray will be back on Tuesday by 3:00 p.m.

May 3: Operated last night; a kid came in from Leone for general peritonitis, but he died two hours later. Miss Anderson and Miss Smiling had a quarrel last evening over the operation; I had a chat with them this evening. We'll be operating again on Tuesday, a hydrocele case. Have a small operation tomorrow.

May 5, 1915, Tutuila, Samoa: Operation yesterday, did one in less than ten minutes, worked like heck all day. There was a show on the Malas last evening. Glick wanted me to go over next door with him, but I had been in bad company and could not blacken my good name. I will go over this evening if nothing happens. Old McCarty fell off the water wagon last night. Was rather a shock to all hands.

I expect to be transferred back to God's country in two or three months now. How that thought is cherished and pondered over! No one can understand without spending two years in Samoa. I have almost begun to have dreams of a little place in old Texas called Bradshaw. I can hardly realize that I may return in the next boat. If my relief arrives on the next boat, I have orders to sail. Hooray! Have taken out the pictures of familiar faces to have a look–the ones locked up a year ago.

Was over to see the fair ones last evening and had a very pleasant time. Mrs. Parham, Mrs. Fare, Miss Massey, and Miss Marvin were welcome visitors; also, it was a jolly crowd as Dr. Parker, Mr. Parham, and Mr. Fare were all in Manua. Murray returned from leave today. Thank God!

May 14: Nothing of importance happened in the last few days. I was over that way once or twice the past period. A very good trip when you have become acquainted. United States have been in turmoil for a week over the disaster of the sinking of *Lusitania*.

The Lusitania *was torpedoed by German submarine (U-boat) without warning on May 7, 1915; over 1,198 persons lost their lives and, of which, 138 were Americans.*

Almost got myself in bad with the fair ones last evening. I mentioned the fact that I had not written home since October. The whole damn tribe was up in arms. If everything turns out all OK, we will sail for Sydney on the 22nd. Governor has ordered our accounts closed on the 20th. Hoping and praying.

May 16, 1915: The ball came off last evening. Sure made a . . . of myself. Took Miss Gass and Miss Massey down as promised to dance them up anchor and away. Glick tells me they are waiting for me with kitchen utensils and a general line of firearms. Lord, how I dread the ordeal! Hope no one is around when it comes off, particularly none of the ship's company. I got part of it yesterday with more coming. Miss Massey forgave me fully. Have not seen Miss Gass yet. Hid all day yesterday.

May 18: Met them *all* yesterday, received a nice letter on manners. Going out to dinner this evening at Mrs. Thiger's; the fair ones will be there. Had a nice chat with Initia last evening. We operated this morning on a club foot patient.

On May 22, 1915, the tug boat USS Fortune became the United States Naval Station Tutuila's station ship.

June 2, 1915: Well well, have sadly neglected my little book the past few days. Steamer arrived Sunday a week ago, no relief aboard. Received word that the *Princeton* is leaving in September. Suppose I will return aboard her. Glick and Pop had a scrape a few days ago.

The General is on the sick list consequently, and things are so quiet. I have been hopeful that his recovery would be detained for another month or two. Received two letters from home last mail—everyone doing very well. I hope to be back for Christmas. *Princeton* went to Leone today. Skinner and Lena will be married on Sunday. Another *Genaw tau*, have not been over to see the fair ones for several moons. Don't like their life very well myself. However, the general is getting all sails up with Miss Gass.

June 10: Glick is still on the list. Have been on watch every night and day for the last few days; however, don't mind it so much as this is *Tele Tigae'* the *Falunailau iego Tui* was *ilooga* for *mata mata aua anapo*. Had three deaths this week due to meningitis, pneumonia, and croup. Lanham will come back for duty tonight. Ship is supposedly going home in September. Miss Anderson would be leaving this boat, provided her relief arrives, in fact, more sanguine than probable. Flugers and Pratts are going home in this boat. The nurses have been doing duty at the other place for the last two weeks. And we have not been over since Mrs. Slayton was operated on. *Here* is for a more successful future forever.

June 18, 1915: Lanham is doing duty with me at present. Steamer comes on Monday—no relief for anyone. Expecting the *Fortune* any day now; the *Princeton* is going home in September. I don't know as how I will come out on the return trip. I have been having a bunch of *togas* with us for the last few days. Hope to be well before the return trip.

Nothing of importance had happened since last writing. Had quite a nice time at the club this p.m. Played pool all evening last two games.

June 28: Things getting along very well, considering going to have a big track meet on the 4th but don't expect to enter on account of my illness. Suppose Slim Brunner will carry off the honors. However, I expect to enter in a ball game between the H'S and Yeoman. Expect an easy victory!

July 15, 1915: I sure have been busy the past few weeks. MCM (Steward) took a ten-day furlough, leaving me the whole dang hospital, including the nurses' ward to take care of. The drug store occupies quite a bit of my time; also, have not had a decent night's sleep since he left. About twenty patients to take care of; two or three have died on me, but I did my best at any rate. We take in on an average of $115 dollars on fountain, not including the drugs and sundaes. Was somewhat surprised when Dr. Parker informed me I was capable of handling such a vast business; did not think he placed so much confidence in me. The steward's duties at this place is not a toy merchant, believe me, combined with the store care keeps one hustling.

Oh, by the way, Mrs. Slayton died last Sunday night! The nurses are back to duty at last. I planned a little horseback ride with them yesterday with a purpose in view. I got them all off OK and started with Pendleton to the falls, following not far behind. Heard the steward was returning from Leone. I told them I would go ahead. They did not know the trail, so I did not find them. My dream did not come true. Met Miss Gass, Miss Pendleton, Miss Smiling, and Miss McEron. Pendleton dismounted, and I had to take Gass for a ride. The point is I did not go to the falls with Pendleton as I had planned—dang it all!

There is trouble brewing today for last night one gallon of whiskey was stolen from the dispensary. Governor detailed about fifty men to act as "Master of Arms" to discover the thief; so far nothing has been reported. Irwin gets the blame for it so far.

Well, have just returned from the side of a corpse to finish this little periodical, a consumption (tuberculosis) patient died just now. These things do not trouble me anymore—my nerves are as steady as steel. You soon become hardened to death. Upon my arrival at this place, I was a little nervous after watching them crash in but no more. Steward returns on Friday—thank the Lord! Have three operations next Tuesday. By the way, gave my first anesthetic the other night. Expect to help MCM next Tuesday in administering the lines.

July 16: Things moving about as usual today, no change so far. Made arrangements with Pendleton to go to the falls again tomorrow afternoon—hope to meet with better success than previously mentioned.

So far, no one has been convicted of the robbery mentioned yesterday. Nevertheless, some of them are pretty scared; besides, there is strong circumstantial evidence pointing toward a few of them. Steamer is to arrive next Monday, this is Friday. Glick is going home on her with a medical survey. According to all his symptoms, he has *Phthisis* Pulmonary Tuberculosis. Poor cuss, he has not been out of bed since the fight he had with young blood, which I mentioned some time ago. Some claim this to be a direct cause of his illness.

I had a nice little walk with the little girls last Saturday. Steamer arrived on Monday. Received a few letters—everyone well at home. The long dry spell has broken at last. Worked like the dickens yesterday during a hell of a downpour to keep the houses from flooding. Still raining this morning and expect a month's rain now at the least. Glick left Monday for God's country—sure wish I was along with him this a.m.

Quite a few suns have passed away at my coming. Everything smooth as expected. *USS Nanshan* will arrive on August 10 and will leave on 25th and land in San Francisco about the first of October.

Had a ball game last Wednesday and had a very good game. Will play again tomorrow. Can't think of anything to write as I am impregnated with the thought "Homeward Bound." Inspection this morning, and we all handed in our uniforms and standing by to go home. Lanham found out the inevitable last evening. I turned her (Pepe) back over to him. Things moving all OK, had quite a score the other evening. The two girls and I went out for a walk and did not get back until after dark. I stopped off at Akin's office when the girls came in. Upon my arrival, Miss Pendleton came over and called up the CMAA (Chief Master-at-Arms). However, she only wanted the boat.

Fai mea ma Sinister Anapo. Talala mamua. May try *Inetea neii Polula.* Tealaega went to Nunlu today, mother is very sick. Worked like hell today. Made out all my monthly reports and started my books off for next month.

Have an operation tomorrow. The boys are taking up a collection for the homeward bound today. Went out to the falls yesterday and had quite a nice time. Denny and I posed for a picture; he must be the pretty one. Ask Akin as he took it. Whoopee!

August 18: *USS Nanshan* and *USS Fortune* arrived today; relief for all hands aboard. Strange to say, I am not as keen to go as I had expected. There is something canny the way these enchanted islands grasp a man's higher feelings for civilization. Nothing but constant thought of home brings me out of my lethargy. We expect to leave on 20th or 25th.

Gusted, a man I knew at the station, came down also. They tell me that he is somewhat of a booze high-tester nowadays. He is trying hard to bring a fall out of it, but the last few nights have not succeeded.

I will sail for Magdelena Bay from here. Everything is stirring, preparing for homeward voyage. Ship is strictly regulated now that Commander Ellis took command on Tuesday. Bulgaria almost started something a day or two ago.

When the war erupted in August 1914, Bulgaria was recovering from the negative economic and demographic impact of the recent wars and declared strict neutrality. During the summer of 1915, when the military balance swung in Germany's favor, Bulgaria committed to the Central Powers (Austria-Hungary and the German empire) in September 1915 and declared war on Serbia the first of October.

Richard, the new hospital assistant, opened his heart and told me a secret that I almost told Miss Viola Gass. McEran came over scared to death and explained everything to hubby, and he, in turn, proceeded to investigate. I have old Ananias bested in this one case. It is somewhat of a romance, *however*.

Played ball today with the *USS Fortune* team, and at the first part of the third inning, they quit. Score one to eight. Don't blame them much. Old Slim sure was tossing apples. I tried my luck at catching today, did better than I expected. *Fortune* is going to Manua tonight.

Well, this is my last night here. Went to the picture show and came back with the girls. Told them *tofa* (short for Talofa, phrase for "good-bye"); will go to the ship at 5:00 a.m. The boys almost got me in bad last night. They drank up all my alcohol, then put water in the bottle. I sent it up to Miss Snelling, and she tried to burn it; then she carried it up to the doctor, and he said a few things.

Miss Gass and the girls sure hate to see me go. Initia gave me a ring and a bunch of flowers from a few Samoa fans. I am a little sorry to leave old Samoa, for I have had a pretty good time here, considering everything. I had not moved for one year–arrived in January 1914 and left Tutuila, Samoa, Pago Pago, United States Navy Station on *USS Nanshan* on August 25, 1915. Came aboard *USS Nanshan* at 12:15 p.m., sailed at 1:00 p.m., and took my last look at old Samoa. Left from midstream–I did tell all my *iagas tofa* that I will not regret the parting.

August 26: Passed Union Island late this evening–weather fair.

August 29: Weather continues fair, we are about 740 miles from Samoa. Going to call in at Washington Island–will not stop at Flannigan Island.

September 3 at sea: Had quite a squall on Tuesday. It has blown over now, and weather continues fair. We will arrive in Honolulu on Sunday if nothing happens. No happenings worth noting. As of this evening, we are living on hard tack (biscuits) and rice; we get it three times a day. Coffee is clear as water; going to put in a supply when we reach Honolulu. We have been at sea nine days today.

September 5, 1915: Weather fair, sighted Honolulu at 6:00 a.m. this morning and arrived at 1:30 p.m. Hoping to get a ball game, going with someone. Land sure looks good to me after this long siege of water. However, the thought of a seven-course repast is the predominant thing in my mind at the present after eating rice and sloop for the past twelve days.

September 8: Have been ashore for three days now, having a ripping good time. Got an auto and traveled over 400 miles in six hours. Saw much of the height rise off Hawaii. I met Dr. Duncan. Glick was the first man over the gangway upon my arrival. He was operated on here for liver abscess; he leaves tomorrow through Samoa.

September 14, 1915: At sea, weather is fair, have just passed out of a storm that we fought for four days. Will arrive in San Francisco on Monday, if fair weather continues—can't arrive any too soon for me!

September 18: Arrived in San Francisco, had fair weather in all latter part of voyage. Went ashore last night with Slide, saw the entire Samoan Siva troupe, and had a good time in general.

September 19: Was ashore with Red Irwin, Keeland, and the rest, went out to the fairgrounds and had a very enjoyable time.

September 20: Were transferred to training station last night. I am doing duty insulation camp tonight. Went ashore in Oakland this afternoon to see Toe, who is in Canada, and Mabel is in Los Angeles.

September 23: Have to go to school for apprentice tomorrow. Don't know whether to desert or not. Put in an application for Las Animas, Colorado Hospital this a.m. and took eleven days' leave. I should be back in a week or two.

September 24: Dodged around all day to keep out of school. Slept in isolation shack but was supposed to sleep in barracks.

September 25: Went to school this afternoon. Was put in ward with typhoid suspect this p.m. and will not have to start back to school until he is well—I hope. Steward is doing all he can for me. Hope to get out of this damned hole soon. It is worse than Samoa.

Las Animas, Colorado Hospital

OCTOBER 30: WELL WELL, here I am again . . . got away from the station at last. But just in time, for I was sure going at some pace. Toots is on the way to Hopkins; the *Princeton* is in Bremerton, Lanhan is at Mare Island, and Irvin is at Bremerton, Washington, but by now, I expect he is on his way to the east coast. The old *Princeton* crew sure is scattered. I read my application one day and left on the next. I just barely had the $$$ to get here. Adams, Tucker, Lee Fadden, and Kelly are about the only people I know here. Went ashore last night, but I don't think much of their liberty town. Pretty dull, pretty dull! I hope we will get a basketball game team started soon. They have a good football team here, but I can't play that well. Time for the movies. Will try to write more tomorrow.

Things are a little livelier since I have become acquainted. I am on the football squad. I practiced this p.m. and all days from three to five. Had a game matched with Las Animas, but they got cold feet and backed out. They are trying to get a game with La Junta for Sunday. Hope we succeed. Heard from Toots some time ago, he hasn't sent the money yet. I am trying to get home for Christmas–can't say any success so far. Have not heard from any of the old *Princeton* boys yet–expect to hear soon.

I wrote a number of long neglected letters this evening. Ducky and Dutch have gone to Los Angeles. I am doing duty in surgical ward. Some work–to get another man tomorrow. He just arrived from San Francisco and was at dinner.

November 12-15, 1915: Everything is pretty quiet. Have a football game with La Junta. We travel up there. I am not positive that I am going yet. Hope to at any rate. Wrote Green and Glick a letter but don't know whether I will get the money or not.

November 16: Went up to La Junta with the team and had some game . . . six to seven our favor. Quite for the last two days; have another game with Las Animas on Friday. Pretty sure I'll get to play with them. Stand by to take notes at a postmortem operation this p.m. Have almost decided not to go home for Christmas. Did not get to go to practice this p.m. No mail from home yet.

Things progressing about as usual; had quite a bit of fun at practice yesterday and attended the movies last evening. Received a card from Alie a day or two ago.

November 23: Thanksgiving Day is approaching. I've got one hellish hard football game to play.

November 27: Everything is moving quietly. Played football on Thursday and won three to zero. I wrote quite a few letters today. Received letters from Glick and Toots–they both want more time on their loans. Heard from home, and everyone is well. I am having a pretty good time; it snowed a little this morning.

December 4: Am doing night duty. Paid today.

December 9: Still on night duty; had one death since I went on. I have again resolved to work on my correspondence studies today with my first lesson tonight.

December 12: Well well, I am still at my studies and have sent in the spelling lesson that I failed the last time. I think I am on my way for good . . . I will try at any rate. After I get my degree, I can always use it anyway. Stoner has gone to town tonight. Suppose my partner Wygal will stand his watch as usual tonight. I should have some mail at the post office. I have not been over to check for a couple days; haven't heard from Toots or Glick, yet, so no money! Well, still on my studies, sending Arithmetic Part 4 this morning. Received a letter from Glick; Irvin is in Chicago, and Lucky is in St. Louis.

Christmas Day: This is certainly one heck of a Christmas–just about equal to last year in Samoa. Wonder what they are doing in those obscure islands this morning! Sure would like to be back. I haven't received a darn thing from home yet–don't expect to, either.

December 31: Have completed four lessons since the ninth. I will endeavor to send in at least four lessons every month in the future. I am working on spelling part *four* and letter writing part *three* at present. I received a box of candy from Mama–heard nothing more. I have certainly concentrated my time for the past twenty days to studying. I am going to order an encyclopedia this month provided . . .

January 1, 1916: USN Las Animas Hospital, Colorado. It is New Year's Day. Resolutions adopted as following: discontinue playing pool and bowling; stop smoking in all forms; buy only one-dollar worth of movie tickets per month and use other money to go for books. These rules I will have to adhere to as my financial need is something astonishing.

January 9: Haven't received any news from home and don't know whether to go home in March or not. I am working on my studies yet.

January 22: Things very quiet—nothing important since last entry. Still working night duty. Spindle is with me now.

I completed Algebra Part 1 and Arithmetic Part 6 on 1 January. Oh! By the way, broke every dang one of my New Year resolutions!

February 4: Finally received a number of letters from home. Fair and carnival begins here tonight. I am trying to raise funds for a band. Ordered a new *Webster's International Dictionary* today and hope to receive it soon. I have decided to go home in March, provided I hear from Toots. He is now at Training Station, Goat Island, situated in San Francisco Bay.

February 16: Received my dictionary today, also a letter from Effie. We are trying to promote a minstrel show, but as in trust, it is somewhat lacking, and so I fear the results are not going to be satisfactory.

February 18: Ordered my encyclopedia today, hope it will arrive soon. Received a letter from Toots yesterday and was greeted with the astonishing fact of his marriage. Suppose it is another $50.00 deceased. This makes over $300.00 I have lost through supposedly friends since my enlistment.

February 21: Old McCarty raised hell last night—didn't get much sleep. Spindle left on a ten-day furlough this morning. The minstrel show comes off March 14-16. Had a Hawaiian singer and dancing troupe through last evening. Received card from Osus this a.m. Diamond promised me the laboratory in the first of March.

February 22, 1916: The Office of Military Administration in Apia wrote to Resch and Company, Brewers, Maitland, Australia, that "they must procure for the men absolutely the best quality beer that is on the market at the lowest possible price . . . we have tried almost every brand that is on the market here. What better advertising proposition can you have in Samoa than this? The soldiers, if given the opportunity, will lay a foundation for the Resch in Samoa, which would remain long after the war" for Mr. August Resch, the brewery's proprietor and a prominent German Australian, however, did not save him from being detained as a prisoner of war.

On February 22, 1916, the first class of Samoan nurses graduated from the United States Navy Nurses Training School in Fagatoga, American Samoa. Act of Congress in 1908, an establishment of the Nurses' Corps, selected twenty women as the first members and assigned to the Naval Medical School Hospital in Washington, DC. They became known as the Sacred Twenty, and in 1913, Navy Nurses saw their first shipboard service aboard the Mayflower and Dolphin.

February 29: Sloan, poor old fellow, is getting kick this a.m. although he seems to worry less than anyone. Ducky was restricted for thirty days yesterday for dictating to an officer. He's taking my detail tomorrow. Expect to get a call for eleven o'clock this a.m. over some of last night's treatment.

I heard from Mama yesterday. I am keeping my studies up fairly so-so. Declining a little of late, however—Spring weather! I think I will get my encyclopedia by Saturday. Pay-day Saturday. Finally, got off night duty last Saturday and assigned in the laboratory now. Blew up the distillery first thing on Sunday; however, QC did not hear of it. Had several urinary tests this a.m. and spent the day on sputum (phleyen) and other daily routine work. I made a better feces test this p.m.

Punkin came back yesterday. Two of the baseball players arrived a day or two ago. Heck of a sandstorm, blowing the last two days. Have not heard from Effie for some time—can't imagine what is wrong. However, don't care! Hope I never get another!

March 9: Made another one of those infernal urinary Wassermann (test for syphilis) today. Going up to La Junta tomorrow to see the "Birth of a Haitian"; borrowed coins to make the trip. Received encyclopedia yesterday, and it is sure a nice set of books. I heard from sisters Bell and Bess today.

March 10: Made the trip to La Junta without a mishap, also met a pair of charming ladies. The picture was unexpressive but simply superlative, the music producing three quarters of the effects.

March 13, 1916: Doing duty in lab, working pretty hard.

April 2: I am going to take the exam for STD (Sexually Transmitted Diseases) in a few weeks. Was recommended this quarter and don't know how I will come out, but a chance on anything once is my motto. Expenses are more than my salary again for this month.

April 10: Made ten Wassermann tests today, twice over, but still they are not accurate. I will have to make them again tomorrow. Received no news from Toots yet, expect a letter next week. Have a little doubt over playing ball, I missed practice today—too much work.

April 24: Baseball was too fast for me—had to drop out. I am instigating another team. Miller, Tat, and Burris left today for the West Coast. I jerked a muscle in my leg a few days ago and believe that it will put a jinx on me to play the first team but will have a second chance.

Was in to see Dr. Barber, he has arranged for me to spend two more years here in laboratory.

Well, little book here, we are once more; however, I am not in the same mental condition as the one in which I wrote the precious page. After all, I am sure it was merely a passing fancy, and I am glad of it—got it off my mind at any rate.

I had a very good time while at home but not as enjoyable a time as I had anticipated. Things are somewhat changed. I returned back here expecting to find a football team underway but no such thing—there will not be any football this year. Have been working like heck the past few weeks. I put in an application for recruiting duty yesterday. I sure hope it is approved and here is one thing: I promise divine providence to save my money and attend a school of some kind while on duty. That is one thing I sure am going to adhere to—I swear it and *Toe saw Ale tusi lelei, Au sowe a ole 'fufu' Amoua Au Lei.*

December 7, 1916: The letter (application for recruiter duty) returned disapproved. I darn near decided to ship over several times but have now made up my mind not to. Bob is in ICU. Heague Wood was transferred to Mare Island. This pay, I put away twenty dollars, I must save thirty-five dollars out of December salary. Received letter from Mama today, and she says to send home all the clothes and such stuff that I don't want. I took my discharge from Royal Roller and caught the 11:03 train on January 17, 1917. I have been in Oakland, California for about a week now, staying with Earl and Mable. Haven't started work yet, don't know just when I shall start.

Reenlisted in United States Navy

MARCH 10, 1917: AGAIN do I make note in my little dairy. Since my last notation, I reenlisted in the United States Navy on February 5, 1917. Served quite a few days at the United States Navy Training Station and now here I am on recruiting duty at Los Angles, California. Went out and worked one day in a coal mine but soon changed my mind about the navy. She is not so bad after all. Believe me, I am going to stick with her for the next few years at any rate. On the sixth of March, delivered Selden Mitch here—wife sore as the dickens.

March 18, 1917: I have been here almost two weeks now. I met my old friend, Plato, who now has a very desirable position with a brokerage firm here in California. Have found Dr. C. H. Howard, one of the finest doctors I have met in the United States Navy, contrary to the report I received from Duncan.

I received my dictionary from Morris Cope. Have a registered letter in Oakland, which I can't figure out the meaning of. It may be a trap to catch me in a stunt I once pulled. Selden left last Wednesday.

March-April: Have been getting along very well the last two weeks. Like the duty first rate. Still stopping at 711 and Figueroa and was out to the Children's Hospital with the landlady's (Mrs. Mylin's) daughter. I had a few lines from Cassidy; he seems to think the letter may get me into a joke yet!

May-June: Still on recruiting duty, although I came darn near getting off. Have to go to San Diego with Spike to take the examination in a few more days. I don't expect to make it but the examination is imperative. I was in San Francisco last Sunday and had quite a nice time. Heckdom and I took up a bunch of recruits. Failed to see Buster for he had moved. I am having *Mona lava mo ole tigo lea inie mabe Ole tiga la milea tale tupa.*

The German steamer Elsass and SS Staatsekretar Solf interned in Pago Pago Harbor on August 6, 1914 shortly after the outbreak of World War I and which was signed by the United States Navy; the officers and ratings are taken in Pearl Harbor. The steamer Elsass was towed from Pago Pago to Pearl Harbor on May 17, 1917 by USS Ajax, which was turned over to the United States Naval authorities in Hawaii.

On June 15, 1917, the 350-ton German steamer SS Staatsekretar Solf that was assigned by the navy on April 7, 1917 and recommissioned as the USS Samoa, following an overhaul at Pago Pago Naval Station. The first United States vessel to bear the Samoa name was armed with four 3-pounder semiautomatic guns.

It has been pretty warm once or twice with the temperature reaching 104 degrees. I have been visiting the beaches, and also the cabarets, quite frequently, of late. Old Matt and Clark are on their way to France, or perhaps, have already landed. Morris is in San Francisco. Dif Lanham is in the civil service down at Linda Vista Hospital, Los Angeles, California.

July 13: Returned yesterday from the southern city, San Diego. I journeyed there to engage in a little mental struggle in order that I should sit among the August body of First Class (PhM1c). I haven't the least idea as to whether I am going to gain the converted seat or not. Trusting in God that I will as I want to make one more step before long. I am very seriously considering another step which does not pertain to my naval career. Meanwhile, I will calmly wait with unselfishness . . .

Sister Nell got married in either April or May–I have forgotten the month. Received a letter from my esteemed brother, Guy, who also was about to step into the army. Had a letter from an old friend, Tip; sometimes, I wish I was in his boots. He was a lucky dang fool if he knew it. I received another letter from Possum, who is coming out if nothing happens and trust that it will not.

September 16: Since last entrance, Guy has been enlisted and deployed. He is now at the Naval Station 9, San Francisco. Old Tip has reenlisted; I suppose he is at Mare Island Naval Hospital, California. Old Spike was transferred to Savannah. Carl has again gone on one of his periodical trips to nobody knows where, and my kind sister, Mabel, wrote, asking me to keep away from Oak. I have decided on a nuptial alliance with Jo McKinnes on the first of the coming month.

I was out to hear the celebrated Billy Sunday and from what I heard, I am unable to see *why* he is a *celebrity*, provided last evening was a fair sample. But they are all fairly running over one another to shake his hand.

William Ashley (Billy) Sunday, an evangelist–was a gift athlete that left baseball (Chicago White Socks) and engaged in Christian ministry. During World War I, Sunday was a supporter of the US war efforts.

Made a trip to the island of Catalina—another celebrated resort, which, in my mind, is a fluke. The folks at home tell me there will be a cry *little field crop* this year, again—same old story.

October 1, 1917: Miss Josie "Jo" McKinnes from Indiana and I, eventually, succeeded in getting ourselves married, which was quite a different task. Reverend J. J. Meyers performed the feat. After quite an exciting time of searching, we found a little bungalow. Earl made us a visit last month. Morris has just succeeded in getting himself engaged.

November 1-17, 1917: Received word today that all hospital crewmen and those recruiting duty are soon to be detached.

December 3: My telegram came today to go to the *USS Saranac* for duty.

December 5: Jo and I left Los Angeles on December 3 on the 3 p.m. train to El Paso, Texas and onto Abilene, where a merry sandstorm was the first thing that greeted us. It was cold as a beagle there. We caught the A&S Flyer to Bradshaw, Texas.

December 9: We left Bradshaw for Chicago. We returned to Abilene onto Ft. Worth, Texarkana, Little Rock and St. Louis to Lafayette, Indiana. We had a very good time at home, or would have had, if not for the infernal sandstorm. George brought us up from Bradshaw. Sister Bess was the only one not at home. The train from Abilene was late by two hours.

December 10: Trains were all late by twelve hours in St. Louis. Jo and I arrived in Otterbein, Indiana on December 11, about 6 p.m. Mort and Maude, Jo's "sister," met us at the train station.

December 13. We left Otterbein this a.m. Jo traveled to Chicago with me, and we stayed overnight at the Morrison Hotel.

December 14: Left Jo at the station and then speeded eastward on the Manhattan. Arrived next morning in New York; New York is a hell of a city in my opinion. I came over to the Recruit Ship this day and I must say, some ship! For the first time in my life, I had to eat with Negros ("niggers" epithet used freely during that era). I couldn't get over to the *Saranac* for some time yet.

USS Maryland on September 15, 1915.

Coal mine crew at Hells Hiuyes. L-R:
third to the right, back row, Walter Irvin with pipe.

Josie (Jo) McGinnis Irvin at Coronado Beach—Walter and Jo spent the
day here while Walter gave typhoid shots to some navy boys.

A detention camp—a period of temporary
custody prior to custody order.

Men's Infirmary, Naval Hospital, Las Animas, Colorado.

Officer's Infirmary, Naval Hospital, Las Animas, Colorado.

Baseball team, Naval Hospital, Las Animas, Colorado.

L-R: Walter Irvin, on left in the second row.

USS *Saranac* Brooklyn, New York—Amid Uncertainty

J ANUARY 5, 1918: REPORTED aboard *USS Saranac* on December 18, the ship will be in New York a few months. Jo and I just returned from a trip to Indiana and have an apartment in Brooklyn. We had a very enjoyable visit at Otterbein, Indiana. I couldn't get back there for Christmas. Spent the day aboard the good ship. Just received word from Mama saying Guy had finally got home and was married on December 26, 1917.

January 13, 1918: Still sticking around the *Saranac*. Weather is very uncomfortable–zero! The coal storage is becoming serious in New York.

April 16, 1918: The *Saranac* was supposed to have been completed a month ago, but we are still here. She was being converted from a steamer to a mine planter at South Brooklyn, New York. Probably will be more than another month before we leave. I worked on the stores for the past few days. Bob has been put into Class One, and Vollie in Class Four. Guy came over a few days ago–don't know where he is going. He is on the *USS Mallory*. Morris B. Cope is still at Los Angeles.

May 12: Guy is on the *USS Mallory*. Jo went home today and I am about as lonesome as one ever gets. Don't know when this darn tub will leave here. But *here* is hoping it will be soon!

May 25: Left Shewan dock on May 23 about 4 p.m., anchored out in bay, and started trial trip at 4 p.m. next day. I have not heard from Jo since Wednesday. No unprecedented happening so far and have started back.

May 29: Laid in the bay for three days, taking on ammunition and stores. Left at 10:00 p.m. last evening and headed for the north, I think. It rained all night.

May 31: Had a little gun practice off Province town. Mass today. The *Saranac* dropped down to President Roads and anchored in view of the famous all-state statue cornerstone laid by President Taft.

June 2: Still lying in Cape Cod Bay, making speed tests. Sure wish I could get ashore.

June 5: Arrived in Boston, Massachusetts Harbor on June 2, and we are here yet. Have been taking on store mines, and so on, and anchored close in the first two hours, then beat it for the outer harbor. No shore leave for everyone but CPO's (Navy Petty Officers). Boston seems to be quite a pretty place. We just escaped the submarines as news came of their action on the second. We were within the zone of operation a few days ago.

June 10: Still hanging around Boston. Jimmie and I went ashore yesterday, first time for me, since we left the twenty-third of last month. We were out to Revere Beach, a place something like Coney and Venice. Today, I received a letter from Jo; I suppose she is on her way to Los Angeles by now. I sure do hate to have her go, but I know she wants to, so that's enough for me. I certainly do miss her.

June 13: Still lying out in the harbor. Get liberty when we want it, but I don't want it. Received a letter from Jo—she is on her way to Los Angeles. I've changed my mind: I suppose she will be better off there.

June 17: Left Boston Harbor yesterday at 5:35 p.m. I did not hear from Jo. We are out in the deep this a.m. and headed east, going where I don't know. They have taken away all our mess tables, and we are eating off deck.

June 18: No excitement yet! Had a sandwich today—the first thing I've eaten since leaving Boston Harbor.

June19: Sea rather rough today. Von Stuben, Austrian-Hungarian Navy, was fired at only 150 miles from us yesterday. No submarine yet, though we have been out three months.

June 21: Ran across a trawler yesterday, who refused to hoist her colored flag. Fired a shot across her bow, and she had to hoist her colors. Have a scarlet fever put aboard tonight, and I am not feeling so darn gay over it either. Sea is moderately rough, today and yesterday.

June 23: We are still on our way; weather is getting cooler every hour.

June 27: At sea. No submarines sighted so far. *USS Saranac* received a message on June 24 to be on alert as one submarine was reported on our course. We've been having continuous daylight for a week now. The northern lights are a common sight for us now. Today is my 24th birthday. I celebrated it by giving my first general anesthetic during Turnbull's neck operation.

We have crossed the Atlantic and are going into Scotland somewhere, I believe. Sleeping with life preservers for two nights past.

June 29: At sea. Everyone is happy, and all's going fine. We will arrive in the morning *if* no monster of the deep alters our plans. Convoy met us this morning about two o'clock that consisted of seven torpedo boats and one destroyer. There is also a balloon zeppelin with us that makes one feel little more comfortable. We've been traveling through the Orkney Isles all day and are still in them.

Entered Invergordon last evening; sailed about 5:00 p.m. There is a bay here. The place was once a Naval Base for Great Britain's Royal Navy. It is a very pretty country. Cromarty Highland, Scotland lays at the mouth of Cromarty Firth, five miles from Invergordon on the opposite coast–an arm of the North Sea at Scotland. The voyage took thirteen days, lacking any significant events sailing the European waters.

I may go ashore this p.m., understanding that now we may not have as long to stay here as we first supposed. I only hope it is true–this dang war is getting my goat. We ship coal tomorrow. Some of the boys went ashore tonight. Gave a thousand dollars to see my Frau.

July 3: Still in place. Went ashore the last two days to practice baseball and played a game with the *USS Shawmut* team today, who beat us eighteen to three. We have only practiced two days, so could not expect much–I may play another game tomorrow. I pitched three innings today. Invergordon is a very pretty place. One peculiar thing is that the women all carry sticks. Very few autos, but a million bicycles. All the women ride bicycles too.

USS Saranac detachment consisted of USS Shawmut, USS Aroostook, and USS Black Hawk, which crossed the Atlantic to Scotland to begin several months of mine-laying as part of a squadron that erected a vast antisubmarine mine barrier across the North Sea. At first, some officials looked upon this as impracticable, mainly on account of the immense amount of material required and the lack of mine layers available. But these difficulties were overcome, and the British and American authorities agreed upon the plan, which was put into effect successfully. In October, United States Secretary, Daniels, revealed that America devised a new type for anti-U-boat barrage. Many plants made parts and that years' time was saved by quality production. Twenty freight vessels were employed. It was to be the biggest ordnance mine project ever taken and a vitally important factor in the antisubmarine campaign. Rear Admiral Joseph Strauss USN, a former chief of the Bureau of Ordnance, was in command of the Mine Force aboard, and Captain R. R. Belknap was to direct the Mine Planters for the battle of the Atlantic.

The eastern part of the North Sea was dominated by Germany and both entrances from the Atlantic were dominated by Allies. The island of Great Britain lies across the western part of the sea, giving the Allies a most advantageous position for blockade. Germany has no ports on the open ocean. Political boundaries are important in war as are terrains features, which constitute abstracts to the free movement of troops, and the railways, roads, and waterways are useful routes of military communications.

July 4: No baseball today, only room for two teams on the grounds as another team had preference. Both the other boys are ashore, so I've had duty all alone today. Wrote a couple of letters to Jo. I sent Adam things to write as the censorship regulation does not permit. Had a boat race. Don't know how they came out. Suppose they lost. I think I will be able to tolerate life away from Jo if I can get ashore to play ball every day. God, but I sure miss Jo. I wish the Kaiser (Germany) would cash in. Trust next fourth of July finds me back in the good old USA.

July 8: Read mail from the States on July 5—one letter was from Jo while she was in Salt Lake. Played ball every day, and we have got beaten every time so far. Have played no official games yet. My arm is on the fritz. Haven't played myself since the first day. Understand we are to go into dry lock soon, wish to God they would send us back to the States for it. I get more disgusted with this place every day—would have been all OK if my arm had not gone on the bum. Went ashore yesterday to practice and saw the game between *USS Princeton* and *USS Quinnabaug*.

July 10: Nothing happened yesterday. Played ball with the *Quinnabaug* team today and defeated them by a score of ten to one—our first official game! The doctor goes over to Baltimore in the morning to hold exam permit for CPHM (Chief Pharmacists Mate).

July 12: Comme need studies for CHPM yesterday. We are getting ready to make our first trip. Loading mines all day. They are all ready for firing too—believe me! Think we get mail today; I received quite a number of letters.

United States Mine Squadron, North Sea

JULY 1, 1918: WE anchored away at 1:00 p.m. a convoy of *thirteen* destroyers—*USS Black Hawk Mine Force Flagship*, its Captain R. C. Bulmer, Mine-Squadron One, *USS San Francisco Squadron Flagship*, its Captain H. F. Butler, *USS Aroostook*, *USS Baltimore*, *USS Canadaigua*, *USS Canonicus*, *USS Housatonic*, *USS Patapsco*, *USS Patuxent*, *USS Quinnebaug*, *USS Roanoke*, *USS Saranac*, its Captain Sinclair Gannon, and the *USS Shawmut*.

July 14: We are off for our first trip—don't know how long we will be out. In number 2 area of the North Sea, a convoy of thirteen destroyers proceeded to sea in two columns. At left from front to rear: *Roanoke, Housatonic, Quinnebaug,* and *Baltimore.* Ships to right are from front to rear: *Canonicus, Canandaigua, Aroostook,* and *Saranac.* It is the most magnificent sight I have ever seen since I enlisted confronts tonight and that is a convoy of about fifty-one vessels ranging from the largest battleship on down. They are four and five deep all around us. We feel important. There were thirteen of the United States ships and they sent fifty to guard us.

As the great ships filed out of Scapa Flow, the form line slowly disappeared in a haze as they swept off towards the southeast. We laid the *first* mine at 10:58 a.m.

July 16: We are at present in the Inverness. Lost convoy in the fog and returned to the harbor this morning without them. The *USS Roanoke* went on the beach.

July 17: Nothing happened of importance today. No liberty Inverness. Coal ship loads mines tomorrow. Troops and crews of the ship had valuable training in quick loading and unloading. We have *three* more trips to make in the North Sea. Laid sixty-five miles of them; last trip one mile deep. We are laying them all the way across South to North.

July 19: *Saranac* anchored at Scotland, still lying inside the Firth of Forth (S-Scotland river flowing about 116 miles to the Firth of Forth, an inlet of the sea). I suppose we are waiting on a supply of mines as we've been here now for three days. I'm on crutches, owing to a bruised foot—can't say that I enjoy it either. We've had no mail for almost a week now but think it will be here tomorrow, usually get it once weekly.

July 21: Mail came today. Jo is in Los Angeles at Mr. Crane's. Played ball yesterday with the *Black Hawk* team and lost two to zero. Inverness is quite a city—compared to Invergordon. We are going to load mines tomorrow; guess that means another tryout on Tuesday. News from the western front is a bit more encouraging lately. Wish to God it was over; I'm getting lonesome and tired of this damn war game.

July 25: News from western front continues encouraging. Received mail yesterday from home; Jo and Nellie seem to be getting along OK. Have a pair of nuts in the sick bay. One has pneumonia, the other has a fractured rib. When either laughs, there is pain, so naturally both of them exert themselves to make the other laugh–incidentally, I get a few laughs myself.

I've been studying chemistry the last few days–think I shall take the exam for chief before long. Rumor has been floating around ship that we will be back in the good old USA by Christmas. God knows, and I hope it is true. I've had quite a few chances to go ashore but have only been once. I believe the scenery here is the most beautiful in the world. I thought we were going out Friday, but they have given all hands liberty, suggesting we aren't going out for a while. I received a letter from Spike.

July 27: Nothing of importance happened yesterday. Played a game with the *USS Patapsco* and beat them with a score of five to four. I did play today; beginning to think I'm a back number in the game. My arm is still on the bum. I wrote Jo a letter today.

July 30: At sea. Sunday was spent aboard repairing for trip. On Saturday, we went on our *fourth* excursion. We left on Monday at 2:00 a.m. and had our first excitement when we passed in between two German mines. Later, the ship ahead of us swept one mine up. We commenced lying this a.m. at 9:20, finished at 11:35. We are out on our way back now; presume we will arrive about 12:00 p.m. tomorrow. It gives a person some serious time for thought–*this constant realization of lurking death.* I suppose though, after another trip or two, we will be used to it. At 6:00 p.m., heard an explosion few minutes ago; one of the Limey (British) convoys got a sub. It is the first time one has been around to our knowledge. Have had excellent weather this trip so far, but the fog caught us last time on our return trip alone about midnight, that was when we lost our convoy.

July 31: Came in last evening without a mishap, I believe we are going out again Sunday. It seems as though they expected an attack last time and more than expect it this trip. Here's hoping they hit after we've planted. Read an article in the *New York American*, where Sir Eric Giddles claims the English are planting the mines across the North Sea, or they are doing exactly what we are doing–another English conceit. We are back at Invergordon. Was over with the ball team this p.m. for practice. I'm trying for third base now.

August 2: Still lying in at Invergordon. Nothing happened the past two days. Loaded mines today. I played ball this p.m. with the *Aroostook* team and had three to eleven score–their favor. I am still out of the game with bum foot and bum arm, and today, I've a boil on my nose. I have lanced it three times today. Nose has had me on the bum for the last four days; however, she is about well this a.m. No trip yet, heard that we only make one more. No mail since my last.

August 8: Learned today that the Huns (nickname for the Germans) have been into our mine fields. We are expecting morning attack this trip, up anchor at 1:00 p.m. My nose is all healed over at last. Had me a bit worried for a few days.

August 9: *Fifth* excursion, subs were around last evening about dusk. Quite a number of bombs dropped. Don't know whether they got one or not. Started mine planting about 8:00 a.m. but we are going back to port with ours aboard. Seems tube–something seriously wrong. They were exploding in chains this time. We were fired at last evening by a sub but missed by a hundred yards.

August 13: Still in port. Got back without mishap. Mail came the first day we got back. Jo seems to be getting along OK. Had a ball game. *Saranac* lost as usual! There is some talk of a long trip soon–don't know where or when.

The mines apparently are a failure. Sure hate to leave without finishing whatever we started. On the western front, news is still encouraging. Sub or mines, got the *USS San Diego* in the States. German (U-156 shells) shells Nauset Beach in Orleans, Massachusetts on July 21, 1918.

Huns armed position three miles of Orleans, Massachusetts, when a U-boat surfaced and started firing on an unarmed tugboat and the four barges it was pulling. Torpedoes set it ablaze and wounded some of its crew; everyone was rescued by the skill and courage of the coast guardsmen.

We ship coal today. Diverse *kind of rumors* are floating around to *where* we *are* or *maybe* going such as Breast Mediterranean, Newport, the States, and a few more places. Hope we leave here. I have my application in for CPHM, so should be able to take the exam in a day or so. Counseled myself and prepared now as I will ever be.

August 14: Played ball with the *USS Roanoke* team this p.m. and lost again. Mail came today and received a fat letter from Jo; thought it was news–opened it to find it was nothing but a bunch of funnies cut from Los Angeles' newspapers. Some disappointments–believe me! Quite a gale blowing tonight, glad we're not out. There will be an athletic field meet over at Dingwall tomorrow. I think I shall compete in the one-hundred yard dash. Allies are still going over on west front of 37,000 prisoners, 100 guns, and 10,000 machine guns. I have heard nothing of the wild runners lately.

August 17: Went up to Dingwall on 15 to the Seaforth Festival–rather a rotten place. I met Drewing, who is to be transferred. I also learned that my old friend Irvin is up there. I tried to get up, but all the bicycles were closed for the day. Took us about half a day to get a bite to eat, then the red-headed mutt was as cross as a pig without a mud hole.

All the ships are loading mines, so presume we will be leaving here for another trip. Jimmie is going to a boxing contest to compete. The winners go to London to box. Don't believe the lad has much of a chance.

The board has been appointed to give me exam; am waiting to be called now. I have about given up hopes of getting back to the States for another year or two. God, but I would like to get back. Get more disgusted with this little village each day.

Heard from Jo–the oat and corn crops have brought more than she expected, with excellent prospect for a big crop this year when the oats are all shucked. She is planning to take a business course. Belle is still having trouble with her appendix. Old Wayne is on his way to France. Don't know why I haven't heard from Earl. Guy has made three trips across. Brother, Leak is in Oklahoma now in harvest.

August 18: All the other ships went out today. I haven't the least idea why we are left behind. I'm getting pretty well disgusted with this infernal hole. The boys tried another ball game with fifteen to zero in the fifth ending, and we quit.

August 18: Received mail yesterday. Belle has had her operation at last, and Jo is staying with her. There is about a sixty-mile gale blowing tonight; sure glad we are inside. God, pity the poor sailor on a night like this. News on the western front continues favorable. We take mines tomorrow, going out Sunday or Monday.

I dream of Jo most of the time. God, I would like to see her. Damn the Kaiser! I'm quite a bit worried over her staying out there alone. I imagine a million things happening to her. Usually know all her letters by memory in a day. May God protect my girl; only he knows how I love her.

August 26: Nothing of importance happened since last entrance until today. Up anchor for *seventh* excursion match at 3:10 p.m. Sailed for an hour without mishap, then had a breakdown—one of the *fishes* went wrong and delayed us for forty-five minutes. At 6:25, the circulatory pump broke down, and here we are at 9:00 p.m., setting here as still as a mouse in the path of the Huns subs, not knowing when we will get under way or at what moment we will get a bump in the stern sheets. Oh yes, I saw my old friend Irvin a day or so ago. Frye is also up there; his little girl died. Toots was in Scapa Flow on the bridge last winter.

We are trying to get back to Inverness on one-fourth speed. We reached Inverness without further trouble.

August 28: The fleet came in about 6:00 a.m. Have not learned how many mines they lost. Had expected to get mail today but we were disappointed as none came. Made a liberty last night with Hampton and George; quite a number of amusing incidents during our quest for Sergeant Frumenti (old-fashioned spirits). We followed false clues for an hour and eventually wound up buying tea and a rotten steak. An old gentleman at the commercial has promised us a quart tomorrow. Tried to bribe the barmaid but to no advantage; however, we persevered.

September 1: Played ball on 29 and beat *Black Hawk* team with ten to seven in thirteen innings. Team had quite a reception upon our return. All hands and the skipper manned the raid and cheered like mad. The gang was very much astonished as this was the first interest anyone had shown in the team. Mail came on the 30th. I received only one letter from Jo. Met Jack Diamond at the ball game the other day; he arranged for me to take the exam tomorrow. I am a little apprehensive as to the outcome. Although I may get through all OK–I doubt it. It is rumored that we are going south in the near future. Hope it proves to be true as weather here is very disagreeable. The Allies are still gaining a little on the western front.

September 3: Well, finished my exam at last. Quite a grilling, I admit. I worked on it all day yesterday and today. Think I can get through everything but *History* and *Geography* hit me pretty hard. I am back with the ball team.

September 6: Went over to play ball yesterday, came near getting picked–heaved it up. Belle is out of the hospital. Jo is well. We are eating white bread once more. In the outer harbor, will sail sometime tonight. J. J. Brown was busted to first class CL. I will not hear from papers for two weeks. Dr. Wilson is on leave.

September 14: Had an uneventful excursion last trip–sighted enemy only once and lost quite a number of mines as usual. We have been in Invergordon since our return. Started out to play ball several times but was not put into the game. The boys lost every game they played here. Rumor has it we are going south from here before long. Hope it is true for I am darn tired of this place. Today, I received word that I passed my exam all OK; received official word of it today.

March 1918, Colorado. L-R: York–Pharmacy 3,
Latwood–Pharmacy 1, and Cassidy–laboratory men.

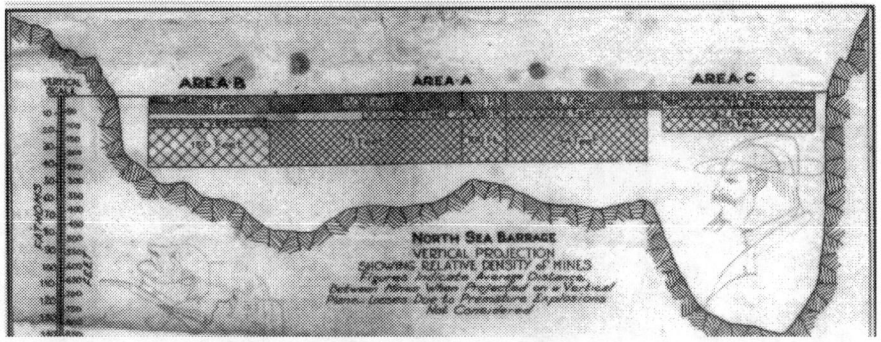

North Sea Barrage map showing relative density of mines.

Captain R. R. Belknap–Mine Squadron.

Captain Sinclair Cannon commanded the *USS Saranac*.

Invergordon, July 1918.

Part of mine fleet anchored in Mary Firth.

Column one steaming out of Mary Firth.

US Minelayers steaming information, 1918

USS San Francisco Flagship–Mine Squadron One.

USS Shawmut

USS Houstonia.

USS Quinnebaug.

USS Baltimore.

USS Canonicus.

USS Canandaigua.

USS Aroostook.

Looking for air bubbles from *F4*.

Tender–a warship that provides logistic support to submarines:
U164, *U124*, and *USS A L 2*.

U124

Fifty mines and twenty-four torpedoes.

F4 submarine

Scene at mine Base 17, Invergordon Island, Scotland.

A torpedo-shaped protective device with erode
teeth in its forward end used underwater by a ship in
mined areas to sever the moorings of mines.

Yankee Mining Squadron.

Mine explosion, "Premature" 22 seconds behind layer.

US mine layers and a British cruiser in a Scottish harbor–1918

Type of submarine mine used in laying "North Sea Barrage."

Attack.

British Destroyer Fleet throwing smoke screen to protect the American Mine Fleet, sailing through North SEFI.

Fueling at sea.

Dry out after long siege of battered weather.

Coaling ship.

USS Olympia–Admiral Dewey's Old Flagship in harbor at
Invergordon, Scotland that just returned from Archangel, Russia.

USS Saranac ship crew—Northern Barrage.

Winners of tied-leg race.

Walter crossing the finish line.

Walter crossing the line the last time.

Chief Pharmacist Mate

SEPTEMBER 16: WE HAVE completed a string of mines across the North Sea. There were two large limes (nickname, for when the British used to sail around, they would take limes (fruit) with them to eat to prevent scurvy) with us last trip. Aboard ship last day is 50 degrees; having a bit of regular weather today. No mail since last writing.

September 18: Nothing worthy to note for the last two days. Have a ball game today. It is windy as heck. No mail. I moved down to CPO Quarters yesterday–a bunch of nuts–these CPOs. We are to go out tonight, I think. Don't suppose we will get back to the States for at least a year. That's the latest dope. There are *always* rumors of some kind.

September 21: Left Invergordon about 11:00 p.m. on September 19 for *ninth* excursion. Submarines reported on our course but encountered none. Morning of the twentieth had a very pleasant experience–a submarine was sighted, and the destroyer fired on her, then threw a smoke screen around the fleet. Heard afterward they were taking pictures.

I am on the verge of losing my cap. Captain Coffman got drunk on someone's alcohol. Blackie and I am accused. The doctor gave me hades. If he presses charges, I know I will lose . . .

Will reach Inverness tonight. Had a submarine scare and smoke screen. Returning trip was successful according to reports.

September 26: Received mail while in port this time. Jo is doing OK. Bob is on his way to Nashville, Tennessee; drought had ruined the crops at home. *Saranac* is on its way out again. Just lost a man—C. B. M. Anderson—overboard; this dampened the cheer at the mess. We looked for him for over an hour. Captain Gannon takes a reprimand for dropping out of formation.

September 29: Laid mines without mishap on the twenty-seventh. Very successful trip, anchored at berth to Inverness for first time. Majority of ships taking on mines this a.m. Do not expect mail before Wednesday. Have no news from the western front yet. *USS Baltimore* returned to the States on the twenty-sixth—Oh, you lucky devils!

September 30: News came today from Bulgaria's unconditional surrender. Crew did some tall yelling. The pessimist that I am, believe it is the beginning of the end.

Bulgaria was forced to accept an armistice on September 29, 1918. The formal conclusion of Bulgaria participation in World War 1 was later punished for its part of World War I by the Treaty of Neuilly in 1919, which the country had to return all occupied territories (assigned the southern portion of the Dobruga region to Romania, a strip of western territory, including Tsaribrod and Strumitsa to the Kingdom of Sof Serbs, Croats, and Slovenes Yugoslavia), and the Aegean territories gained in the Balkan Wars to the Allies, who turned them over to Greece at the Conference of San Remo in 1920, cede even more of its land to pay heavy reparations. The country had been led for a second time in half a decade to a national catastrophe for which Tsar Ferdinand 1 assumed responsibility, abdicated and left Bulgaria to his heir Boris III on October 3, 1918.

We coaled ship today. We are going out again on Wednesday. We received a circular letter today, asking for volunteers *to man two travelers* to try out our mine fields. They did not request a PHM, so there is no chance for me to become a hero. Hope to write off Germans' defeat before many more months.

October 4: We left Inverness on September 26 at 6:00 a.m. for *tenth* excursion; no excitement so far. Lay mines in about thirty minutes. The news on western front is the best we have had. Hope it continues, for I want to see my sweetheart so bad that I could almost cry. So here is hoping Turkey and Austria have surrendered when we get back.

October 6: *Eleventh* trip laid mines without accident; ran into a peach of a gale on our return. *USS Quinnebaug* was disabled and put in at Kirkwall (biggest town and capital of Orkney, off the coast of northern mainland, Scotland). *USS Aroostook* and *USS Shawmut* left for Newcastle to dry deck. We came in next; gale still blowing this a.m.

October 7: No mail. I went to Invergordon today for my clothes. Had one devil of a trip, wet all day; this is the most miserable country in the world. Old King winter is coming—wind blowing—raining continually—dark at 5:30 p.m. Now Kaiser (Germans) is asking for peace today.

October 12: Mail came on the tenth. Jo is going to move. Belle has gotten her school at Corning, California. The folks at home are having a devil of a time.

We are on our way with *twelfth* excursion to plant mines. We just passed three *Limey* subs. It was rumored that the Wilhelm

Kaiser II (Commander-in-Chief of the German Armed Forces of Northern France) had abdicated in favor of his grandson when we left; hope it is true. *Saranac* just anchored another trip without an accident. According to today's rumors, we have two more trips to make. Kaiser offered a peace, but Allies are in doubt as to his motives. There has been nothing done. I would welcome peace—believe me. There seems to be very small chance for an early cessation of hostilities. Make another trip this week to Invergordon.

October 17: Received mail. Jo is going to take a room. Bell is going to Corning for her school—would give million dollars to be back. In Bradshaw, crops seem to be the best in years.

No peace—Turkey is expected to surrender soon. My prayers that it would be soon! Folks at home are on their last legs—wish I was back where I could give them a hand.

October 21: Received mail on Monday. Jo is at Corning, California, with Belle. She likes it fine. We have an influenza epidemic; had twenty-eight men transferred in seventy-two hours and twenty are ill with it now. Working like the devil; MPHNS has been in bed last two days. Hell rising throughout fleet, and army too.

The Allies are still waiting for Kaiser's answer. There may be peace on the way. I am growing another mustache; will send Jo a picture as soon as it gets a bit longer. YMCAs and all the others are all closed down due to the flu. They are going to have a signet ping made as a remembrance of the mine squadron.

Great Influenza Pandemic of 1918

OCTOBER 26: AT SEA on *thirteenth* excursion: had been having a very enjoyable time the past three days. Mines chasing one another around the deck with a sixty-mile wind blowing. The convoy got lost in formation and gone all night. Influenza epidemic is over. Have only five cases left. Ship doctor is still on the sick list with it. I haven't been able to get much sleep lately. *Saranac* is going to Newcastle this trip.

The influenza epidemic killed more people than the Great War (World War I). The war in Europe was winding down at the time of epidemic outbreak. 1918 would be remembered as an unforgettable year of suffering and death and yet a time of peace. An estimated 43,000 service men mobilized for war in Europe died of the influenza. One-half of United States soldiers fell to the influenza virus and not to the enemy. Even President Woodrow Wilson suffered from the flu in 1919 while renegotiating at Versailles for a treaty to end the World War. One-quarter of the United States and one-fifth of the world was infected with the influenza.

October 27: At sea; weather is calm once more. Some doubt to our destination, perhaps, Invergordon. October 26 at 5:01 p.m. laid last mine within six miles of Airdrie, Scotland, in this trip. Rumors say two more trips to make, and then we are to go south.

October 29: In Invergordon this trip; have mines aboard and are to leave at 6:00 a.m. Nice and windy today. Mail came today and yesterday. Vivian is sick. Jo is getting along splendidly. Brother Bob is going back to Bradshaw; he has been sick for some time.

Austria has sued for separate peace. Allies are still going strong. Germany has answered Wilson's last inquiry, and my hopes are high for an early peace. But . . . Germany is still there. So . . . At any rate, I feel better than I have for some time past. I am getting over the reaction of my homesickness. I have been ashore twice in the last month.

November 2, 1918: Turkey has surrendered. Have been ashore twice in last month. Orders of this trip have been delayed, probably waiting for Germany's answer to armistice terms. Trust that she will accept. However, as it requires the disposition of their fleet, I'm very apprehensive. The mess continues with the same gang of nuts. I have written quite a number of letters lately.

November 2: Austria is no longer a fighting power. King Charles I has beaten it. There are now hopes of my getting home. TiZA-Court assisted today. Republic decreed today.

November 4: Austria signed Armistice yesterday. That leaves Germany alone and the bets are that she signs armistice this week. A letter from Jo yesterday; she is having a very good time.

November 5: Pay day–very little to report. Germany is expected to accept Allies' armistice term. We had landing party today. We are standing by to either unload or drop our cargo. Expect to be back in the States by Christmas.

November 9: Had quite a happy hour the night before when the admiralty officers sent out the word that an armistice had been signed. All hands went up in the air—it was of short duration as it was a mistake. However, we are all hoping it will be signed before 6:00 p.m. on Monday. The council met yesterday, and their time expires on Monday. We are still standing by in Inverness. A number of the boys have bet that the *Saranac* would be on her way to the States by December 25, 1918.

I'm getting a bit lonesome for mail. Almost a week now since I had a letter. We should be out of here before the expiration of this month for *somewhere*.

November 11-12: According to last night's report, the armistice has been signed. Hostilities cease at 11 a.m. on November 11, 1918. *The Versailles Treaty* was signed by representatives of Germany and the Allied Powers in the Hall of Mirrors in the Palace of Versailles near Paris, France. The World War was over.

German envoys returned through airplane. Kaiser and CP abdicated some time ago. Prince Rupprecht of Bavaria has gone also. Germany Navy under Red Flag; Germany signed and ceased armistice. The hostilities ceased today; received word at 10:10 a.m.

The flag of the German Navy and merchant fleet was black, white, and red. This flag was decided to be the national flag in 1871 and continued in use until after the fall of the monarchy. A black, red, and golden flag was adopted as the national flag of modern Germany in 1919 during the Weimar Republic. It was a tricolor, consisting of three equal horizontal bands.

November 13-17: We are taking mines off today in preparation of going back (I think). Mail came on the twelfth of November. There is nothing to report during the past week, just standing by for emergencies. Rumored again that we are going home—curse these rumors anyway, for they keep me in a state of mental anguish from day to day. It should be a felonious crime to start them. Expect mail today—don't suppose it will get here, though. All things go wrong for *us* of the mine squadron.

November 21: Received mail twice in the last week. Jo is taking a few intellectual courses. Day before yesterday, we had admirals' inspection. Crewman Goodrich broke his back. Captain called up and informed us we were going back and that we leave around the twenty-fifth through twenty-seventh. We have to take back a load of mines.

November 23: Admiral's wife has been aboard the *USS Saranac* lately. *Saranac* came through without a blemish. All hands are going on leave soon, one-half on Monday for five days. We are not going back to the States for some time yet. German Navy surrendered their High Seas Fleet day before yesterday (November 21) in the Firth of Forth, to Admiral David Beatty.

Almost had a scrape last night. I was feeling blue, and George tried to kid me at the wrong time. I am still dreaming of taking Christmas dinner in the United States. Everything seems to be going according to plans, in regard to evacuation on the western front.

November 25: Skipper mustered all hands on forecastle and informed us we would be back in one month. Orders came for all men, wishing transfer, to make application immediately, but the captain's writer told me there is very little chance of him approving them. So I am laying low. Expect mail again soon.

November 28: Received mail, and Jo is OK. We were told that censorship was lifted, and I wrote Jo a real letter once more but another message came telling us nothing doing, so it will come back soon. It was a dandy letter too. Some of the boys volunteered to Base 18 Inverness today—a bum line, I call it. All hands are going ashore this p.m. to a show, and then we are to be entertained by the "limes" tonight. Had a very good dinner today, but the chicken needed a haircut and shave! Thanksgiving is gone. Everything is in preparation for free for all Saturday night. We leave Sunday sometime—I hope! Last Thanksgiving Day, I ate a goose which Jo cooked.

November 30: Going to get under way tomorrow at midnight. Will visit Scapa Flow all day Monday; Scapa Flow is a sheltered area of water in the Orkney Islands off Northern Scotland. Then to Bill of Portland on the southern coast of England for about a week there, and then we are off for the United States. Censorship is lifted once more. I will write no more; however, for fear they clamp down again. Well, we visited the German fleet in Scapa; would much rather omit it and go to the United States. Thirty-two of our men left today for the base to do mine-sweeping; thought I would be one of them. Kexderling and Brown were among Toots—these mortals be. The medical doctor is due back tonight—I have been taking inventory today and yesterday. It seems like a dream—the thought of getting back to the United States. But my troubles have only begun—I am not out of the navy.

December 2: Ship headed for Bill of Portland through Scapa Flow at 11:00 a.m. Wacs gave the boys a farewell dance. Expected a huge scrape but it did not occur. Bid farewell to Invergordon at 11:30 last night. Came through the British fleet this a.m. and reviewed the German Fleet also. Some powerful ship but was sadly in a neglected condition; the entire fleet is rusty, dirty, and in a very poor condition. All hands manning the rail cheered. Limies played the *National Air* all down the line, but silence reined when we passed in review by the hums. On the quarterdeck, groups of men in filthy clothes lolled about, hands in pocket, smoking. Swiftly *Saranac* passed the carrion, swung to the starboard, and plunged gratefully into the cleansing clear blue waters in the firth, homeward bound.

December 3: Passed the Emerald Isle today, although at a distance. We have been sailing down the North Channel all day. Some talk of being in Portland for two weeks . . . wish they would change it. Are to pass Sicily Isle tomorrow at 5:00 p.m.; we're in sight of the coast at all time.

December 5: Arrived in Weymouth, England at 10:45 a.m. and anchored in the outer harbor. I was seasick all day yesterday. A leave was granted to 350 of the crew. Expect mail today. All leave to London has been changed; only forty men can go. We are near Portland prison-the great English Penitentiary.

December 8: Nothing of importance to mention in the last three days. No mail since last entrance. The doctor returns on Tuesday, and Andi leaves for London the same day. Latest rumor says we leave here on the twentieth . . . curses!

December 11: Left for London.

December 15: London is some place! In all my traveling, London takes it. Spent more money than I intended to, got drunk two evenings. Visited the war trophy display at Westminster Abby and a few more places of interest but not as many as I originally intended. There are at least three women to one man in London, and the vice is beyond comprehension unequal in the world. Glad I made the trip, and I am also sorry—leave for the United States tomorrow.

December 17: Delayed our departure by twenty-four hours yesterday but we are at last under way for the dear old United States. Davis reported man aboard at 11:00 p.m. with diphtheria. Had all hands scared and witless for fear we would not get away. He was transferred one hour before departure to the *Bushwell Hospital Ship*.

Mo got one hell of a cussing out for not arising when a Chief Pharmacist Mate called him last night. Oh boy! It is one grand and glorious feeling to get under way once again.

December 18: One year ago, I arrived overseas aboard the *USS Saranac*. Weather is very good—just a bit seasick today. I am praying the Lord I can get shore duty when I get back.

December 20: Stormy weather past two days; made practically no headway. Good weather this a.m. but have been waiting on *USS San Francisco. USS San Francisco, USS Saranac,* and *USS Canonicus* are headed for the Azores now. The remainder continues to United States through northern routes. Some storm—some storm!

December 21: We are under way; calm weather. I have decided to put in an application for duty at Las Animas, Colorado, as soon as I arrive in the United States.

December 23: We dropped ashore at Punta Delgada at 6:00 p.m. No liberty tonight, coal ship tomorrow and leave tomorrow night—just missed the opportunity of getting mail on the boat. The Azores, Isle are in the protectorate of Portugal. Really glad we came this way now as we have missed a lot of bad weather and coaling ship in Halifax. The island looks about the same as all other tropical islands with one exception—all the houses along the cliffs are white. Farms are closely clustered in terraces along the hills as far as the eye can see. I will try to get ashore tomorrow.

December 24: Christmas Eve, Ponta Delgada, Azores, Lord, and 3000 miles from the United States and six thousand miles from Jo. No opportunity to go ashore. Came alongside and coaled today. Will leave sometime between now and midnight. No more stops now until we reach the United States. God, think I'll never again leave without Jo *if* it can be avoided. Bum boats have been alongside, selling booze all day; naturally, all hands are stewed. Purchased some fruit while ashore; however, not enough. Christmas last I was aboard this tub and it was cold as blazes about this time. And here I am again. More lonesome than I was last–never again! There are plenty of booze and wild women ashore according to reports.

December 25: Spent my first Christmas at sea, left the Azores at one p.m. Christmas morning–weather calm.

Another Christmas gone, spent at sea. Very good dinner, considering! *USS Saranac* menu: noodle soup, tenderloin steak with onion gravy, mashed potatoes, peas, sliced tomatoes, coconut layer cake, pumpkin pie, fresh fruit, ice cream, coffee, and cigarettes off Ponta Delgada St. Michguel, Azores.

Learned this day that the crew of the *Saranac* has been lucky indeed; when she left Shewan Shipyard, all the cylinders were filled with emery and nuts in the generators. When she left Boston, there were bets of ten to one she'd never came back, but we are now on our way with no stops. Weather calm–nothing to report.

December 26: Weather calm–nothing to report.

December 28: Weather calm. A committee meeting with the captain's presence.

January 1, 1919: New Year's Day–still at sea. We are 513 miles away this morning. Weather has been very good, so far; if it continues, will be in tomorrow night. I have my request in for transfer to United States Navy Las Animas Hospital. Some of the boys kept us awake about half the night.

January 2: Will arrive at Hampton Roads sometime tonight. Glory is, we get mail tomorrow. Been away from the United States seven months, but it seems like seven years.

January 4: Received a bundle of mail yesterday. Jo is in Otterbein, Indiana. Vivian is much better. I have not been ashore. Did send ten telegrams last night. There was a riot here a few days before we landed. Rumored we are here for two weeks, then going south. Captain R. R. Belknap has gone to Washington for orders. Summerville and three of the other boys were killed sweeping mines. Clearing barrage after the war took long hard hours, working around the clock on a dangerous mission.

Furlough Home

JANUARY 10, 1919: JUST arrived after a twenty-five hour trip from Fort Monroe, Virginia, at the Fowler Hotel in Lafayette, Indiana. I am expecting Jo any minute. Came over land with Best; he got off at Greenburg, the city with the tree growing on the Court House. Came through Chesapeake and Ohio to Indiana, then Big 4 (New York Central) to here, came through Richmond, Cincinnati.

April 4: I have neglected this part of my career for the last few months. Visited Otterbein, Indiana; while there, just stayed my full ten days. I return to find the *USS Saranac* had been affected with a rather severe damage on January 19 after the last mines had been unloaded from the ship; there was a fire aboard the *Saranac*. The fire spread so rapidly that the sleeping officers had to make a quick escape in their nightdress. The men in the engine room were barely able to attend the pumps without suffocation from the smoke. The *Saranac* had gone to Philadelphia Navy yard. I came up the next day, got everything in the medical department off, and in short order, *USS Saranac* was ready to go out of commission.

I laid around for two months, getting myself ready to go to Record Ship Philadelphia, PA. Jo came over a day or two after I got here. The *Saranac* left a few days ago for New York where she went out of commission. I am now at Dispensary 419. Jo is still with me. I asked to be put on the *USS Camden*–very genial bunch here.

The Mine Planter Saranac

There was the Mine Planter Saranac
And she cruised the old North Sea,
In search of the Hun, the son-of-a-gun
Who was looking for you and me.
We only saw two, and that is quite true
And we think they found our sting,
For we planted our mines
And it did them up fine
For they couldn't have missed our string.

USS Saranac

In our mission, the *Saranac's* watchword is "We strive to please"; when success does not crown our efforts, "we cheerfully strive the harder."

From "Walter's Squadron One" photo album
By: Regenald R. Belknap, Captain USN
Commanding Mine Squadron One, US Atlantic Fleet

A Week on the *Saranac*

Monday we will rise at five and *Ki Yi* down the deck,
Scrub and wash gratings, just to please our . . . exec.
Rig in our starboard boom, and coil down all our lines,
Break out our mining tackle, for
tomorrow we load mines.

Tuesday we snap out at five, and eat our scanty chow,
Get ready for a load of pills, I
think they're coming now.
Two hundred in an hour is about our average speed
And DEATH to all the U-boats is
the Mining Squadron's creed.

Wednesday we must coal, you know,
for our boilers must have steam,
Of all the DIRTY, ROTTEN, jobs,
it's the meanest of the mean.
When the last bags in the bunkers,
and your back is nearly broke,

You wish you were an army man; he is a lucky bloke.

Wednesday we will stand by—for official sailing dope,
Hammocks are found crummy, and
the crew breaks out the soap.
Scrub and wash your canvas, wear
your fingers to the bone,
And wonder why you left that place
you used to call a HOME.

Friday is a field day, just to keep our good ship clean,
Wash her down from stem to stern, and
make her bright work gleam.
Holystone the *fo'c's'le* just for exercise, you see,
And after, sand and canvas, clamp
her down with the squiggle.

Saturday get ready for inspection;
all hands be prompt at nine.
Have your flat brushed precisely;
your shoes must all be shined.
Have your uniform quite ship-shape,
for everybody knows,
That the kind of sailor that you are is
shown up by your clothes—your
uniform.

Sunday we will shove off—for the mine fields far away,
Somewhere in the old North Sea, where
the U-boats sometimes stray.

We'll drop the whole six hundred old,
and then paddle back for shore,
And about the same time next week,
we'll go out and plant some more.

Squadron One Album
Unknown

April 20: Was transferred to the *USS Warden* ship from *Record* ship, and from there onto the *USS Hopkins* Navy Yard Philadelphia, PA, where I am now. I met quite a few old *Saranac* pals. The *USS Hopkins* will be here for a few months yet. I shall try to get a leave soon. Have moved; Mac left for New York on Monday, and Jo and I took his apartment. Easter Sunday I spent at home.

June 4: Just returned from twenty days' leave . . . home had a very enjoyable time. The *USS Hopkins* is going out of commission next week. I am transferring to the *USS Chandler*.

June 26: *USS Hopkins* went out of commission on Friday at 3:30 p.m. on June 17. Transferred to the *USS Stewart* and remained there almost one day—left on four-hour notice. Had to leave Jo to get away the best way she could. I came down on the Chesapeake line to Norfolk, Virginia and dashed out to the North Base at Hampton Road on Sunday; left from there on Monday. *USS Kilty* makes a cruise soon to the Mediterranean Sea. Will leave Saturday for New York.

June 29: Arrived in New York at 1:00 p.m.; soon on our way again for the Azores. There was quite a gale blowing last night.

July 5: Fourth July is over—spent at sea—will arrive on Monday in Azores.

July 13: Arrived in Azores on June 8 and left on the 10th. All hands piffled. Bolshevik (Russian) is all around. Arrived at Gibraltar on July 12 and went ashore here yesterday. Gibraltar is a narrow strait that connects the Atlantic Ocean to the Mediterranean Sea and separates Spain from Morocco . . . nothing of importance to see. I cannot get over the bullfight.

July 17: Left Gibraltar on July 15 and was under way for Spalato two days now. Sea is very rough. *USS Kilty* arrived in Spalato on 18 July—nothing important.

Spalato, an episcopal city, is the center of an administrative district in Dalmatia, Austria, and on the Adriatic Sea. Spalato is a striking sea-front.

July 19: Arrived in Splalto on July 18—nothing of importance.

July 31: Arrived in Venice, Italy and assumed the duty of station shop on July 25. Have mail clerk job in addition to all my duties.

Venice is a city in Northern Italy, which is known for the beauty of its setting, its architecture, and its artwork. The city stretches across 117 small islands in the marshy Venetian Lagoon along the Adriatic Sea in northeast Italy.

My enlistment record was changed to duration of war resting today. Oh boy! Soon-soon!

August 17: Have been neglecting my notes for quite a while. *USS Kilty* has been in Venice since the above entry. I went up to visit the battlefield on the thirteenth and had quite an interesting time while there.

We were relieved here yesterday but had to take duty back again as the *USS Cawell* was ordered back to Spalato. Don't know when we will be able to leave this blasted Adriatic Sea (an arm of the Mediterranean between Italy and Balkan Peninsula). I have heard from Jo quite often. Guy finally obtained his discharge. I am expecting mine when we get back to God's country!

August 27: I haven't much to say except that I am darn tired and lonesome, homesick, melancholic, and every other thing that goes with it. Changed captains today; our executive gets the position tomorrow. I'm still worrying with the mail job, in addition to my other duties. Information received today is that in one month we will be returning to the States. No mail for ten days. *USS Martha Washington* is on her way to Constantinople with troops, I think. Conditions are very unsettled there. *USS DuPont* was up here a day or two ago and brought a commissioner for a mandate in Turkey up.

September 28: Almost a month since I made my entry in this. We have been under orders for home about five times since then. *USS Kilty* has been to Spalato to bring mail down to Trieste for oil. Trieste is a city and seaport in northeast Italy; it is a narrow strip of land, lying between the Adriatic Sea and Italy's border with Slovenia.

Hurried to Furme and did an important radio work there for about two weeks. Made a thirty-route trip to Spalato to bring the Flag Lt. back the next morning. That night, we made Venice to get the Flag Lt. to a train for Paris. Oiled and had orders on board to proceed to the United States. Came to Spalato for stores and were to sail that night. Our orders were cancelled from London two hours before we sailed away due to the extremely *critical* situation there. We are stripped for action and under one-hour notice to get away. The Wops (Italians) are due here Tuesday night. When they arrive, we slide out and give them free access to the place. Captain of the *USS Cowell* run them out of Trau a few days ago. The Wops fleet is out of control and roving at random.

They have always been unfriendly toward us, and it seems that they would enjoy blowing up what few (American) vessels there are here. Our mail has been stopped for one month and all hands are in anything but a formidable mood.

October 25, Messina, Sicily: Messina is the third largest city on the island of Sicily, Italy and the capital of the province of Messina. Ye Gods haven't put a line in here since coon's age. Here I am on my way home after all my disappointments; left on the evening of October 23. Made Messina this a.m., I have been ailing all day. *USS Kilty* will leave tonight or tomorrow morning.

November 5 at Azores: *USS Kilty* is ready to get under way for Bermuda. It is a five-day trip and the weather to date is terrible outside. Have been here four days and am trying to get home.

November 16: Just under way on our last stretch. Have been laying here six days; there is nothing of interest except bicycle riding around. Ship arrived in New York on Tuesday evening.

November 27: Thanksgiving dinner served: oyster soup, roast turkey, oyster dressing, mashed potatoes, creamed peas, candied sweet spuds, sweet pickles, cranberry sauce, celery, raisins, spiced and sugar cured ham, cheese, oranges, bananas, ice cream, mince pie, layer cake, mixed candy, mixed nuts, cigars, and cigarettes.

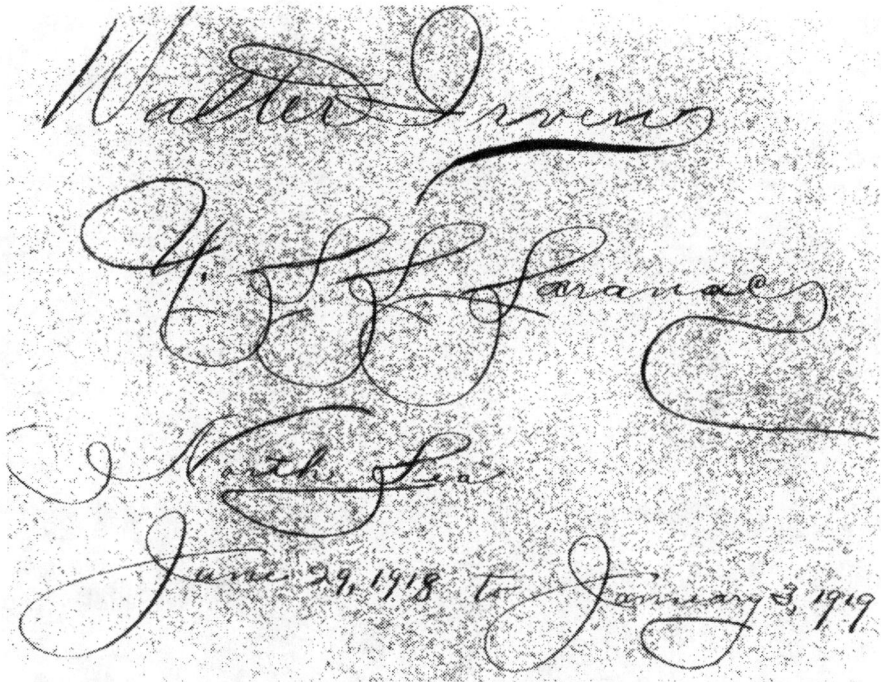

Walter's handmade sign of *USS Saranac*.

Chief Pharmacist Mate sign that Walter made by hand.

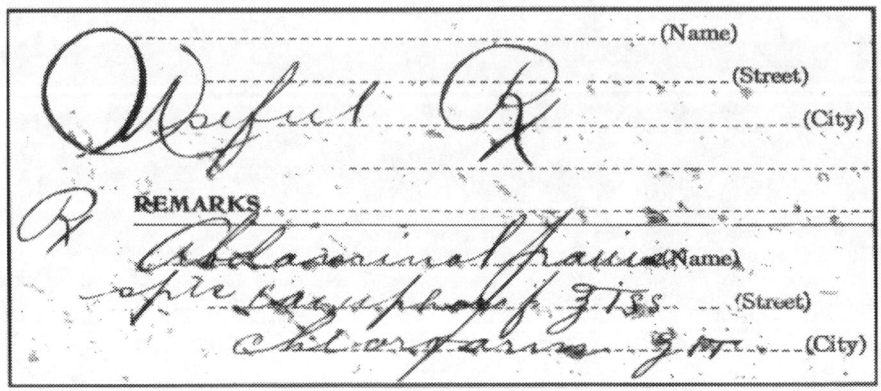

An RX prescription order that Walter had written for abdominal pain.

Chief Petty Officers with dog "Dixie." L-R:
Walter standing at back, five over from the left, with a mustache.

Chief Petty Officers' group.

Walter is in middle of second row with mustache.

Boat deck of *USS Saranac*.

USS Saranac–United States Mine Squadron April 9, 1918 through January 3, 1918–Northern Barrage.

Picture showing European Roman numerals–1899 would be written as MDCCCXCIX, common year starting on Sunday. Roman numerals were used in a method of recording the date.

Sul Grappa–battleground in Italy.

Saluti da Messina. Messina is known as the door of Sicily, Italy.

Gibraltar.

Gibraltar.

Gibraltar.

French waif on board *USS Kilty*.

Venice–King's reception.

USS Saranac after fire.

Submarines *L-4*, *L-1*, and *L-10* at the Philadelphia Navy yard.

A quiet day in the Orkney Islands.

United States Naval Collier "Nanshan."

USS Hopkins.

USS Kilty.

Burial of a fallen brother. Walter Irvin is holding the flag.

Soldiers and navy men with local men of the area.
Walter is holding the flag.

Walter Irvin.

Guy Irvin.

At Last, Walters' Home

W ALTER MUSTERED OUT OF the United States Navy on November 30, 1919 with the rank as Lt. CPhM (Chief Pharmacists Mate CPO Class V-6). Walter's professional qualifications at discharge: Proficiency in rating, Nursing, First Aid, Pharmacy ability, Clerical ability, Leadership ability of men, Conduct, Sobriety, and Obedience, all of which he received high marks beginning at 3.4 to all 4.0s.

Walter, an avid reader, did a lot of studying; he wrote some in Samoan language. Samoan is the traditional language of Samoa and American Samoa, and an official language, alongside of English, in both jurisdictions. He enjoyed writing plays and poems; he was very artistic and was interested in taking photographs. He was also an avid *all around* sports fan and player during his school, navy days, and later times. His diary had phonograph song list of: *When you play With the Heart of a Girl (Heart of a Woman), Back Home in Tennessee, You Can Find A Little Bit of Dixie "Everywhere You Go", N Everything, Piney Ridge (Please Come Back to Me).*

The YMCA, the squadron baseball league, and the track athletics kept men fit and keen; their ashore time was made for lasting goodwill, tended to preserve peace. Sports, music, and outside activities also helped to promote positive image, sense of duty, sense of purpose, and a pursuit of pastime. Most of all, it helped the men to define their lives away from home.

The navy was organized in 1775. There were assigned area for the sick and injured, which had been deemed necessary from the beginning to provide for the care of the sick and injured. The assigned area was designated the *sick berth* or *sick bay*. In the forward part of the ship, the space occupied by each gun was known as a bay. Guns did not occupy some of the bays and those unused gun bays became bays for the sick. When the ship prepared for battle, the surgeon and his mates reported to the cockpit compartment to prepare the area for the wounded. The cockpit is below the gun deck and located below the waterline for protection from shot and shell. As the wounded arrived, their wounds would be evaluated quickly and determine if amputation was required. Due to the absence of any form of anesthetic if amputation was required, the victim was placed on a table and given a suitable amount of rum. Two sailors would hold the injured due to the horrific shock while the surgeon worked quickly. It was estimated that one-third of those wounded died if blood poisoning or infection set in; a sailor's chances were good if he was of a strong physical makeup. Prior to going into battle during the civil war, soldiers wore paper-pin identification. Dog tags were not standard until 1913.

Following a three-week hospital stay with mumps in 1913, Walter changed his rate and started hospital duties immediately. The illnesses on board ship were mostly basically routine as well as the method of treatment. The real health enemies to treat were scurvy and dampness. A diet lacking fresh vegetables and their daily intake of salted meat caused scurvy. Colds and pneumonia were caused from all the dampness.

In 1902, the first Hospital Corps Training School was opened at the Naval Hospital in Portsmouth, Virginia. It provided uniform and systematic training for the new personal entering the Hospital Corps.

The revised structure of the Hospital Corps came by Act of Congress in 1916. The ranks and rates: Pharmacist, Chief Pharmacist, and Chief Pharmacist's Mate, Pharmacist Mate First, Second, and Third Class, and Hospital Apprentice First and Second Class (wore a red cross on the sleeve). The new rate structure title for the petty officers was established as Pharmacist Mate. Walter worked in a wide variety of capacities and locations, including shore establishment such as naval hospital and clinics, aboard ship and as well as primary medical caregivers for sailors while under way. They functioned as specialty technicians that often was challenging. Walter's duties were to take charge of sick bay on board ship, attending to first aid, prepare and administer simple medicines, give anesthetics, medical laboratory, pharmacy technician, minor surgery, operating room technician, and account for hospital and medical supplies. Pharmacist Mates had to have knowledge in anatomy, physiology, medicine, drugs, hygiene, sanitation, nursing, and pharmacy.

IMO (International Marine Organization) regulations require the officer to be fluent in English. The requirement is for a number of reasons, such as the ability to use charts and nautical publications, to understand weather and safety messages, communicate with other ships and coast stations, and to be able to work with a multilingual crew. The officer must be able to transmit signals and receive signals by Morse light (Aldis lamp) and use the International Code of Signals.

Seaman did not hold commission who served between 1903 through 1919, and officers who served between 1914 through 1922. Walter would see the capacity of the Hospital Corps expand during the time he served in World War I and during World War II. More schools were provided for training, and quantifications for advancement in rate were raised.

At the outbreak of World War I in 1914, the Royal British Navy had the most powerful navy. They maintained this superiority until the United States joined in mid-1917. The waterways proved to be a very important type of warfare, with German U-boats sinking any ship carrying a flag of one of its enemies. It was a new age of warfare. Several important battles occurred between large fleets of ships, along with small skirmishes between battles in four or five ships and proved to be important trade routes.

In the nineteenth century, naval tactics found the steam ironclad firing, explosive shells of sailing tactics out-of-date. The *Dreadnought* battleship became the predominant type of battleship; the revolutionary *Dreadnaught* of 1906 was the first battleship to entirely dispense with smaller guns and used steam turbines for its main propulsion. The battleship rendered all existing battleships outmoded because she was larger, faster, and more powerfully armed and moved strongly protected than existing battleships that became known as *pre-Dreadnaught*.

The mines, torpedoes, and aircraft greatly increased the complexity of naval tactics when introduced during the Great War. The gun, though, remained the principal naval weapon, for it could deliver its blows at the greatest magnitude in the greatest extent of various circumstances. The fleet tactics concentration had remained a fundamental objective of tactics until the development of long-range guns mounted in turrets. The nature of naval tactics, the increased range, and field of fire of naval guns change were of specified importance for the admirals for it meant they could now execute focus of fire, rather than direct focus of ships.

The navy imposed the line ahead on sailing fleets for the need to bring ships' broadsides into activation performance. Experiments made during maneuvers by stream navies, combined with the experiment gained in early 1900s, showed that no material change had taken place and found it was still a condition imposed by the physical necessities of the case that this freedom could only be obtained when ships followed one another in a line. This allowed each ship to fire over wide arcs without firing on friendly ships. Steaming with the enemy off the side enabled a ship to fire simultaneously with both the forward and rear turrets, maximizing the chances for a hit.

When in pursuit or flight, or when steaming on the lookout for an unseen enemy, a fleet may be arranged in the line side by side. The pursuing fleet would have to incur its own risk of being struck by torpedoes dropped by a retreating enemy. But the fleet would have the advantage of being able to bring all its guns that could fire ahead to bear on the rear ship of the enemy. When an opponent was prepared to give battle and turns broadside so as to bring the maximum of his gunfire to bear, he must reply by a similar display of force–the line ahead must be formed to meet the line ahead. Each ship in the line generally engaged its opposite number in the enemy battle line.

Different strategies were tried to avoid submarines. At first, ships tried to zigzag to avoid hitting one, but it was found not too effective. Later, light steel nets were hung around ships beneath the waterline to deflect torpedoes. Also ineffective, sometimes a ship would ram a submarine as it surfaced, in which nineteen subs were destroyed. A ship designed to have a ramming capability typically had a tumble-home hull design that would allow the ram to strike below the waterline. The design of hull was inherently slower than almost any other hull design, giving an additional disadvantage to ships employing rams. Ships required to fight end-on when attempting to arm or to rush into a headlong pell-mell battle were designed to give as much fire ahead or at the stern of the vessel as on the broadside. Usually, this was done at the expense of seaworthiness, and in many cases, firing directly ahead caused blast damage to superstructure, decks, and fittings. This was another factor which made ramming invalid as a tactic maneuver. Submarines were shot at, but they were hard to hit before they submerged. The most effective way to destroy a sub was by the use of depth charges. At first, they too were not very effective, but later, depth charges were improved. Placing many mines at many depths on the busy sea routes and to blockade bases proved to be very effective.

The mines, torpedoes, and aircraft posed a new threat, which each had to be reckoned, piloting to tactical developments such as antisubmarine warfare to the use of dazzle camouflage intended to make it difficult to estimate a ship's speed and its headings, and prevent submarines from effectively firing torpedoes. A striking design painting along the ship with long bold lines, frequently cutting across the hull and thus rendering the bow of the ship indistinct was briefly lived as the stark lines intended to confuse submarines; it instead made them a more visible target. The final evolution of camouflage was the prevalent gray shades known as

Haze Gray in the United States Navy. The camouflage war paint was confusion to the eye. The area of the North Sea was patrolled by air blimps and scouting aircraft.

The German forces occasionally employed Zeppelins to attack enemy shipping, but this never inflicted serious loss to the Allied. Zeppelins is a type of rigid aircraft pioneered in the twentieth century and used after the breakout of the war. The German military mainly used the Zeppelin for reconnaissance missions for the navy.

The British and American crew Mine Squadron had laid a belt of mines 230 miles long and 25 miles wide–nowhere less than 15 miles wide–stretched from the Orkney's Island shore 230 miles to the coast of Norway. They were never under fire threat or torpedoed. The Squadron made *fifteen excursion* voyages across the Atlantic, and the British Squadron, *eleven*. A total of 4,000 to 5,000 mines were carried by the squadron on its trip as one load. There were 70,100 mines in all planted, of which, 56,570 were American. Each mine planter carried 24 to 120 tons of high explosive, a total of 800 tons in the squadron. The mine crew never saw any Germans except for the ones that could be seen floating about in the North Sea. There is not much known about the North Sea work on paper because their *Hit* and *Run* game called *Mine Laying* was kept top secret.

The Mine Squadron crew returned home, knowing the *once* questionable *mine task* was done with great execution with committed courage and strength from each member to finish an *ambitious* and *daring* task that they had set out to do. Franklin D. Roosevelt was assistant secretary to Secretary Josephus Daniels of the United States Navy. Roosevelt visited the Mine Force and was quite pleased with what he saw, and Secretary Daniel's annual report stated *the antisubmarine offensive producer of the year.* The effectiveness of the North Sea barrier never went unnoticed. The Mine Squadron had done this *Hit and Run* game task of which had not been done in the world before. Admiral Benson, high professional authority, spoke of it as *one of the most successful efforts of the whole war by any of the forces engaged.*

It took great leadership, making bold decisions and confidence from the *whole* Mine Squadron crew from top to bottom, charting the *footsteps of the messengers of peace.* Casualties were very few. One man fell overboard at sea from the *Saranac* while working with paravanes' there were four other deaths among the 4,000 crewmen. Despite close navigation through mine, swept channels, and near other mine fields, there were neither other deaths nor other injury largely due to the captain and navigator of the flagship. The work was hard but never dull. Ordinary living conditions were uncomfortable for the mine planters' crew, but the men took whatever came with moral strength to resist opposition, danger, or hardship. They knew that to meet the driving foes, there was a task for them to meet, break, and bind.

In the Russo-Japanese War of 1904, mines were used as an offensive, rather than purely defensive, in early defense in early 1900s. World War I torpedoes were largely ineffective. Naval laboratory tests conducted revealed that over half of the torpedo warheads would not fire in controlled tests. Head-on encounters often caused the firing pen to fail, and warhead would not detonate.

Paravane was a weapon used by the navy to remotely detonate underwater mines; there are offensive and defensive paravanes and there are main paravanes and auxiliary protector paravanes. Some paravanes are equipped with cable cutters that cut the moored mines. Explosive paravanes are essentially a towable or controllable mine.

World War I had modernized technology, making use of telephones and wireless communications, armored cars, tanks, and aircrafts. Weaponry use of cannons was positioned in the frontlines and fire. The naval technology warfare saw improvements in alternating and unrestricted submarine warfare in the Atlantic. Germany deployed U-boats (underwater boat) led to the development of depth charges hydrophones; blimps and Hunter-Killer submarines, along with ground warfare, all underwent a revolution. They deployed U-boat (submarine) after the war began.

During World War I, the navy property in American Samoa, which was developed in 1914, became useful for the United States after Pearl Harbor in 1941. In 1951, with the Navy Base no longer needed, the navy moved out, and Pago Pago became a commercial harbor and port. Samoa Americans joined the military, fighting and dying alongside our veterans in wars. Regardless of weather or foes of the sea, the action of a duty post was never abandoned. The sea was definitely crucial to the war effort and victory for the Allies.

The attack on Pearl Harbor, Hawaii on the morning of December 7, 1941 and the lack of any formal declaration prior to the attack, led President Franklin D. Roosevelt to proclaim December 7, 1941 to be a date which will live in infamy. The attack was intended as a preventive action in order to keep the United States Pacific fleet from influencing the war that the Empire of Japan was planning in Southeast Asia against Britain and the Netherlands as well as the United States in the Philippines. The attack consisted of two aerial attack waves, totaling 353 aircrafts, launched from six Japanese aircraft carriers.

On September 30, 1942, Walter reentered the United States Navy. His "Navy Continuous Service Certificate" showed he served as a recruiter through May 15, 1945. He was assigned to USNHS Great Lakes, Illinois from October 1, 1942 through January 27, 1943 until he resigned to United States Navy Recruiting Station at Springfield, Mass from April 27, 1943 through May 15, 1945.

The navy has land bases for ships, transports, planes, tankers, and hospital ships worldwide. There are dry docks, anchorages, wharves, ramps, and barracks, and it's a vast fleet of armed merchant ships, carrying weapons across the seas. Bases have a great system of factories, steel mills, arsenals, and ordnance depots. The navy provides a score of the finest training for its recruits. Many pamphlets, booklets, and brochures were handed out for recruits, including themes of travel, training, and opportunity, saying, *Men Make the Navy–The Navy Makes Men.*

In 1944, Walter had spent time on the sick bay, along with six other men: James F. Young, Newport, Vermont, Yeo2c USNR; Maynerd Young, Newport, Vermont, Yeo1c, brothers John Geehern, Westfield, Massachusetts, Yeo2c USNR; Frank Maddox, Cardington Avenue, Pinehurst, Massachusetts, PhM2c; Joe Vler, Main St., West Groton, Massachusetts, PhMC; Walter Irvin, Springfield, Massachusetts, CPhM PA (Chief Pharmacists Mate "CP0" Permanent Assignment); and Dr. F. W. Ripley, Lt., MC USNR (sent to the Pacific).

On May 18, 1945, Walter was discharged from the United States Naval Pier, Chicago, Illinois, at the age of fifty-one. His ratings posted as recruiter was for Proficiency, Leadership ability of men, and Conduct, which he had in 4.0s.

As a young boy, he served his country and yet would reenlist when duty called, no longer that young boy with an aspiring mind. Walter was of a brilliant mind, but his dream of being a doctor was no longer after he left the navy in 1919. He had given it a concert effort. His Navy Pharmacist Mate duty would never be left behind of the talent he knew so well.

Walter Irvin's diary gives us a nostalgic view of a compelling glimpse of values of service and duty from Chief Pharmacist Mate to Lt. CPhM. The changes by assailed advance in technology during World War I is a unique snapshot of a time served on the *USS Saranac* and the other USS ships from time to time. For the sailors' onboard ship, after sunset at 1904 (military time), it meant *dimout ship*. At 1920, movies were shown on the cargo deck of the *USS Saranac*. *Darken ship* was at 2200–sunrise meant–*light-up ship*.

Captain Sinclair Gannon was born in Columbia, Texas. He graduated from the Naval Academy on June 8, 1900 and, after serving two years at sea, then required by law, he was commissioned an ensign in July 1902.

Captain Gannon's earlier career saw duty on board seven different ships. By 1912, he was a lieutenant commander and commanding officer on *USS Elcano*, which operated on the Yangtze River during the overflow of the Manchu Dynast. In 1917, he completed a tour at the Naval Academy and was promoted to Commander. He commanded *USS Saranac* and was awarded the Distinguished Service Medal for duties served. In 1918, he was promoted to captain and commanded *USS San Francisco*. In 1918, he attended the Naval War College and reported to the Navy Department, Washington, D.C. for duty in the office of the Chief of Naval Operations. On July 1, 1935, he was promoted to rear admiral and retired in April 1941.

USN Commander Rear Admiral Joseph Strauss, Commander Mine Forces United States Atlantic Fleet, was in charge of the *Mine Squadron One* mine laying in European Waters. Captain Commander, Belknap, UNS Commander of *Mine Squadron One* was in charge of the actual sea work. He was a very strict disciplinarian and experienced mine-force commander but always fair and well-liked by his crewmen.

When the United States entered the war, *The Mine Squadron* contained only three planters: San Francisco, the Baltimore, and the Dubuque, the latter being a small gun boat. Invaluable as a well-trained nucleus, this force was yet small in capacity; the three vessels together carried just 400 mines. When the project of planting a mine field across the North Sea was taken up, dealing with mines by the tens of thousands, more vessels, to make over into mine planters of larger capacity had to be found, converted, and trained—and all this had to be done rapidly. This worked suffered in the rush, traffic congestion, fuel shortage severe weather conditions of the winter, labor shortage caused delays along with the many other war preparations. In five months', five vessels, aggregating 4,000 mines capacity was completed, and after a month's training with San Francisco, they sailed with her for the North Sea.

Bases were established near the towns of Inverness and Invergordon. The mines were loaded and partly assembled in the United States and shipped to bases by a fleet of carriers. Various factories had been assigned and turned out different parts in immense qualities production and survey was obtained. On base, the mines were assembled, tested, primed, and delivered to the ships of the United States Mine Squadron to plant. Naval technology in World War I was dominated by the battleship.

At the time the United States joined the war, the Navy Department urged strong measures, essentially offensive, to hem in the enemy bases so that fewer submarines might get out, or, if already out, get back. Among the many projects put forward, a new American invention came to the notice of the Bureau of Ordinance, where its possibilities were quickly perceived. A few quiet but searching experiments developed it into a mine of more promising effectiveness than any ever used before, especially against submarines. It gave the United States Navy the definite means to offer for an antisubmarine barrage on the German Coast and elsewhere, and the result became the *Northern Mine Barrage* in the North Sea.

World War I is the least documented wars of history projects covered by military. With the military men and women no longer living in all purposes, added history is vertically gone. Walter's keepsakes, diary, and collections of photographs are priceless to family and history. It all helps to put a face on the World War I *Battle at Sea* and life of a *Pharmacist Mate*.

In July 2009, the *Saranac Laboratory Museum* opened with a new exhibit in Saranac Lake, New York. Walter would have loved the 125 years of science. In Walter's Navy journey, he cared for the ill and the injured. The museum in 2011 retired the exhibit for World War I–*The Great War*. The exhibit theme covered those that served during World War I who endured all the different terrible medical conditions.

It is not known what Walter's work or activities were in-between World War I and World War II. Walter and Jo only had one child, a daughter, Marjorie Irvin McKinney. Walter's job called for the family to move often. Marjorie would no more than get acquainted with her classmates when his job called for them to move.

Walter never owned a car. One can only presume that Walter drove a company vehicle. After World War II, Walter and Jo settled in Otterbein, Indiana, Jo's hometown area. Marjorie would marry a young fella, Harry McKinney, from Otterbein. Walter worked for the Joe McKinney IHC Implement Company, delivering equipment, and Jo worked at the Otterbein Library.

Walter, as in the navy, continued to keep things running smoothly at home. He would walk uptown to order groceries in cases to be delivered at the house. The laundry was sent out. Jo and Walter were both avid readers. Walter read a lot of western stories along with his sports magazine. He would get the sports news that had about sixty-three pages, and after he had read it, he would give it to Dr. Snellenbarger to read. Walter and Jo both had a gift for drawing, especially cartoons.

Walter and Jo had six grandchildren, two granddaughters, and four grandsons. Grandson Rolland McKinney got to spend quality time with Walter. He said that his grandfather was a great cook. He made pies and Texas noodles. Had a green thumb for raising a garden and had both a red and black raspberry patch. Dave John of Otterbein that knew Walter said laughing, "Walter would go out in the winter time and throw out radish seed on the snow and come spring, he would have some good radishes. Walter was a good guy—quite the character!"

Walter raised and sold rabbits in a barn at the back of the house. Rolland recalled that his grandfather could call owls and birds and was quite a whistler. As so many did in that era, he had a real knack for whittling small bits or pare shavings from a piece of wood into objects. As a teenager, one conversation that granddaughter Barbara recalls she had with her grandfather was that she thought her generation was spoiled and maybe they needed to go through a depression. He responded emphatically, "Don't wish for a depression. Ask for a war before you ask for a depression."

Walter with friends Milton Nichols, Bob Snoddy, and Pete DeBruicker would get together and sit around teasing and joking with one another. He would make rounds each day, checking in at the barber shop, the drug store, the gas station, and the post office . . . whistling as he went. His highlight and passion was baseball. He would sit in a lawn chair on the front porch and watch the games being played on the ball field across the street while listening to a game on the radio. After the age of TV, he would sit watching TV with the radio to the side, listening to a baseball game.

Walter would buy tickets to see the White Sox play. He would go with his son-in-law Harry McKinney and grandson Rolland to the "The Baseball Palace of the World" at Old Comiskey Old White Sox Park on 35th Street and Shields Avenue Chicago, Illinois. One can just hear Walter say, "Come on, go—White Sox's!"

Walter never forgot what he had learned while in the navy. Granddaughter Mary Jo Gutwein spoke of Dr. Rutherford years later and said, "He never saw a person so smart that never did anything with it." Dr. Rutherford was a family physician in Otterbein until he went back to Medical School and became a surgeon. Dr. Rutherford, Jake Rhodes, and Pete DeBruicker were Walter's close friends.

To the younger generation around Otterbein was John Rowe; Walter was known as a nice man. John's father, Claude, and Walter were friends. Walter had a gift of befriending others. Walter had a goal, but in the end, it was never pursued. Much of Walter's story is unknown for the period of time lapse through death and time.

Walter seems to have worked through his younger years to make his life full and enjoyable. He was a man dedicated to country and volunteered to serve, which he shall always be remembered. Walter departed leaving so many untold stories as so many military men have done. Walter belonged to the Otterbein American Legion.

World War II group.
Walter is sitting (light color uniform #6) on front row.

Walter is fourth over from left on second row in light color uniform.

Walter (second from left) having a good time
with some of his men, 1942

Walter Irvin.

Walter with mop crew.

Walter Irvin.

L-R: Walter and brother Guy.

Walter with his daughter Marjorie "Irvin"
McKinney and grandson Rolland McKinney.

Walter's dog tag, which was not standard until 1913.

Diary, Mine Squadron 1 album, albums of pictures.

A keepsake item that Walter had kept plus badges.

Walter Irvin's grandchildren had this memorial dedicated in memory for his love of baseball. The memorial is located in the dugout at Otterbein, Indiana just across the street from Walter and Jo's house. On August 19, 2012, the house burned to the ground. It was owned by a grandson and used as a rental.

Love of baseball memorial.

Stone at the foot of Walter and Jo's monument.
Walter served in both World War I and II.

Walter Irvin's *Diary*

World War I Pharmacist Mate

*To Alma —
Best always,
Ruby Gwin*

Ruby Gwin

ISBN: 978-1-4669-5227-0 (sc)
ISBN: 978-1-4669-5226-3 (hc)
ISBN: 978-1-4669-5228-7 (e)

Library of Congress Control Number: 2012914482

Trafford rev. 01/08/2013

 www.trafford.com

North America & international
toll-free: 1 888 232 4444 (USA & Canada)
phone: 250 383 6864 ♦ fax: 812 355 4082

It is the leaders of nations who decide to go to war. It is individual men and women whose lives are forever changed by their personal encounter with war. Soldiers' experience was far from the comfort and understanding of their families. They return home to loved ones, imprinted with memories that impact their body, their emotions, their psyche, and their perspective on life. It is the testimony to human endurance how these men and women and their families forge a way forward, with the memories of war woven into fabric of their lives, creating both frayed edges and patches of strength. Walter, Jo, and Marjorie are one of these families. The images and reflections of Walt's story, while severing his country in three wars, is dedicated to Walter, Jo, and Marjorie and all families whose lives are touched forever by the reality of war.

Paragraph written by Barbara "McKinney" Kerkhoff for the Walter Irvin Family